Sons OF THE **FATHERS**

Sons

OF THE FATHERS

New Zealand men write about their fathers

EDITED BY **BILL SEWELL**

TANDEM PRESS

First published in New Zealand in 1997 by
TANDEM PRESS
2 Rugby Road, Birkenhead, North Shore City
New Zealand

ISBN 1 877178 08 X

Cover design by Jacinda Torrance
Design and production by Graeme Leather
Printed and bound by Kings Time Printing Press Ltd, Hong Kong

Contents

ABLE AT TIMES TO CRY

I

Fathers and sons. A popular conception of their relationship is that of conflict: an eternal struggle, bitter, intense, sometimes to the death. We can trace it as far back as biblical times, to David and Absalom in the Book of Samuel, contending for control of a nation. Readers of Samuel Butler's novel *The Way of all Flesh* (published in 1903) will find it in the semi-autobiographical account of Ernest Pontifex's attempts to free himself from the influence of his clergyman father, the lugubrious and inflexible Theobald. More recently, the struggle has been played out in *Shine*, the film story of the resurrected pianist David Helfgott and his father Peter, the Holocaust survivor and virtuoso *manqué*.

Perhaps we have Oedipus to blame for this conception, or more precisely, Freud, who seized on the legend of that ancient Greek hero to describe a neurosis most of us would otherwise be unaware of. For conflict, directed both inward and outward, is the essence of the Oedipus complex, where the boy wrestles with the father for the mother's exclusive attention and yet feels guilt at this compulsion to oppose a parent whom he should love and respect. No doubt this is the course of some father-son relationships, but it is by no means the only story.

Warmth and companionship are just as likely to be present in father-son relationships. Of course, they may not always be there on an openly acknowledged or uninterrupted basis: the end of childhood can curtail them, while the mellowing of old age can draw them out. A powerful example of writing which portrays warmth and companionship is

Martin Edmond's *The Autobiography of my Father* (1992), a lyrical and intimate 'rehabilitation' of his father, Trevor, whose last years were overshadowed by bitterness and a sense of failure. The book is a mixture of interior dialogue, interview, fragments of the father's writings, and poetic description. Edmond's device of addressing the father in the second person contributes greatly to bringing to life the closeness of the relationship, as in these telling words: 'I do not think I ever saw you cry. If any man had a reason to shed tears, it was you, but I suspect you had lost the ability.'

Not being able to cry must be a characteristic of many New Zealand fathers. Edmond's book is perhaps the most direct examination so far of a New Zealand father-son relationship. But a good deal of New Zealand fiction and biography has explored this territory. It drives a major element of the plot in Maurice Gee's *Plumb* (1978), for instance, and Michael King's recent biography of Frank Sargeson reveals that Sargeson's father played an important role in his life long after the young Frank had fled to his uncle's farm.

As this collection of sons' stories about their fathers sets out to show, there is a great deal of variety in New Zealand father-son relationships. Yet the father-son pairing also generates certain expectations, both in popular culture and in literature and biography. Penny Hansen, in *My Father and Me* (1992), her collection of writings by New Zealand women about their fathers, mentions the 'wordlessness' – or inexpressiveness – of some of the fathers, as well as the fact that father-daughter relationships have tended to develop in a recreational context: at weekends, at the beach, on camping holidays. This is consistent with Jock Phillips' conclusions on the Pakeha family man of the mid-twentieth century. In *A Man's Country? The Image of the Pakeha Male: A History* (1987;1996), he points out that the 'fairly typical middle-class experience' was of 'a hard-working, responsible father who drove the car and provided the money but who played little obvious part in running the household'. His relationship with the children was largely as a 'figure of fun', who 'took the kids to the zoo or out for a Sunday drive'. A corollary to this division of labour is that the family man often maintained the 'man's man' fiction by erecting '[f]ences of sexual segregation'; and, as Kai Jensen observes in his study of masculinism, *Whole Men* (1996), he justified his family man status as a mark of manhood.

II

My experience of my own father is rather different from the stereotype, although it does share some of its elements. My father was neither a New Zealander nor really a man's man. I became interested in writing about my relationship with him through a rather circuitous route, which provides an explanation for the origins of this book.

In 1995, I was invited to write an entry on my father for the *Dictionary of New Zealand Biography*. I was hesitant, largely because I in fact knew very little about the man. I had shared only some 20 years of his life, and for long periods of that time he was not on the scene. I realised, though, that one way or another the necessary material for a brief account of his life was available – in an unfinished memoir written shortly before his death; in the few letters he had left behind; in his published and unpublished writings; as well as in my own memories and the memories of other people who had known him. So I accepted the invitation and set about gathering and reading the material.

Very soon, I had collected more than I needed; and after I had drafted the necessarily skeletal dictionary entry, I was reluctant to abandon the more interesting material. This then prompted me to write – without any particular end or indeed structure in mind – a biographical essay which would at least preserve something of my father's vibrant personality and voice. The only thing I did plan was to approach my father through his role as a much-loved and charismatic university teacher.

As I wrote, however, I found myself taking a more and more active part in the narrative, with the result that it became something of a dialogue between myself and my father, and between my present and past selves. I had slipped inadvertently into examining my relationship with my father, and, in trying to understand him, I was also concluding some unfinished business with him. It was a cathartic and, at the same time, exhilarating experience. On completing the essay, it occurred to me that while my relationship with my father was unique, what would not be unique was my interest in such a relationship, and that other men might also want to chronicle their own experiences of their fathers. This proved to be the case.

On the face of it, writing about your relationship with a parent is a rather self-indulgent exercise. 'So you want to write about your father? Fine, but do the rest of us really want to know?' I believe so, for a number of reasons.

Firstly, we are an inquisitive species. Our inquisitiveness extends both outwards to the stars and inwards to our fears, delights, and our relationships. We want to know what it is that shapes and motivates other people, to hear and read stories of how they feel and cope, whether with joy or disaster or a difficult parent. In the case of the contributors to this collection, their pieces also supply an invaluable historical record, in some cases perhaps even the beginnings of more substantial biographical or autobiographical writings.

Secondly, for some decades now, women have been documenting their feelings and their relationships with family members, friends, and lovers. Men, on the other hand, have only recently begun to break the silences that have surrounded the more delicate areas of the male psyche. Robert Bly's *Iron John* (1990), which sets out to rediscover and reassert a positive sense of masculinity – including the importance of the 'mentor' relationship – has had considerable impact in the USA. Australian family psychologist Steve Biddulph has emphasised the crucial role fathers play in parenting male children in *Manhood* (1994; 1995).

In New Zealand, as my earlier discussion suggests, there has also been some progress towards exploring the male sensibility. But the wider community still seems reluctant to recognise that men have feelings that are worth documenting or analysing. Between fathers and sons feelings can be particularly difficult to acknowledge. No relationship can be more fundamental to a man's conception of his own masculinity than that between father and son. This book aims to throw light on that relationship as experienced by 13 New Zealand men, and to break down some of the barriers to such an illumination.

Finally, although this book depicts some relationships that are less than satisfactory, even damaging, it is also a celebration of the good ones, those that have left both parties the richer. Fathers have much to impart to sons – and, of course, to daughters – anything from instructing them in practical and sporting skills to showing them how to behave towards other people. Perhaps, then, some of the essays in this book can offer models to fathers and would-be fathers, as well as sons, of what it is that makes for successful father-son relationships.

III

This book is not a representative selection. It never set out to be. Two aims guided me in soliciting contributions: first and foremost, to secure interesting and well-written stories; and, secondly, to include a range of contributors. I believe that the first aim has been achieved. The second was always going to be more problematic. An editor of a collection such as this can rarely determine in advance its final make-up. Many of those invited from a carefully devised list decline; then, once there is a full complement of acceptances, it is found to be unbalanced – too many academics and writers, perhaps, and not enough lawyers or sportsmen. Another unintended consequence has been that all the contributors are aged between 40 to 60. But in the end, range and balance are of more importance to social scientists and statisticians, and the intrinsic interest and quality of the contributions is the main justification for their appearance here.

The response to my invitations was excellent. I needed to approach only 43 men before I had sufficient contributors, and, of these, only five chose not to respond at all. I am most grateful to those who did deliver copy. Not only does it rob time from busy lives to write such pieces, but the process of remembering and articulating can itself be very emotionally disturbing, for both the writers and their families. Those who in the end couldn't manage it, or who declined the invitation, have my understanding.

It is interesting to focus briefly on some of the reasons given for turning down my invitation. Predictably, several men gave pressure of work as the reason. Others had fathers – or mothers – who are still alive and would have been hurt by a candid account of the relationship; or they had re-established cordial relations with their fathers after shaky starts or patches, relations they did not wish to jeopardise. Others preferred not to turn their attention to anything autobiographical, either because they genuinely have no interest in the area or because they feared that doing so might divert them from other work. Still others thought that they had nothing of significance to contribute to the topic. One man had no wish to revisit problems that he believed to have been resolved. Another was saving the story of his father for a friend to put into a play. Another felt it would be unfair to his father, who was long dead and would be unable to answer back. Finally, there was the distinguished writer who intimated that it was all rather too much beneath his dignity. Many of the reasons for declining are intriguing in themselves, but they must all be respected, and, in some cases perhaps, the stories will be told at a later date.

IV

Each contributor's experience of his father is unique, and each contributor has adopted a different approach to writing about him. Their contribution might take the form of a letter or a series of vignettes; blend fiction and biographical material; make free use of family papers; express itself in the vernacular; be highly analytical or poetic. But certain general themes do arise from the stories in this book, and it is worth drawing attention to them.

One thing all sons have in common is that their experience of their fathers is fragmentary. We cannot share in our father's life before our birth: in most cases, we leave home long before their retirement, so that their old age is largely closed to us as well. The period spent together can be relatively short: in Tony Simpson's case some 15 years, in Bryan Gould's 12, and in Harry Ricketts' – because he spent many of his early years at a boarding-school – no more than 10. The most extreme case here must be Philip Temple, whose father disappeared from his life when Temple was a toddler, and was not rediscovered until nearly 40 years later.

Such fragmentariness is a factor pondered by many of the contributors, and used by some to excuse giving a one-sided or incomplete view of their fathers. It can be a source of frustration, because it makes our fathers that much harder to know. It is probably all the more frustrating where the father has had an upbringing utterly unlike that of the son. Both Tony Simpson and Greg Newbold have some direct experience of a so-called humble background, and so are able to empathise more easily with their fathers' hardships. But to Nicholas Reid and Harry Ricketts, their fathers' earlier life truly is, in the famous words of L. P. Hartley, a 'foreign country' where 'they do things differently', and of which they are denied all but a tantalising glimpse. Upbringing is also a factor which can account for the disparity in character between father and son, and it is fascinating to observe how wide that disparity can be. Apirana Taylor, careless of his personal appearance, while his father is unable to tolerate 'the littlest speck of dust on his shoes'; Rupert Glover, the successful lawyer, looking back on his father's semi-bohemian existence; and Philip Temple, mountaineer, explorer, and author, with a father long committed to a passive, sedentary existence.

What is also common to most of the contributors – Greg Newbold and Apirana Taylor are the exceptions – is that their fathers are dead. Their death is inevitably accompanied by a sense of loss, whether at the absence of a precious companion or at missed opportunities; and an early death is something with which it is particularly difficult to come to terms. Bryan Gould, for example, regrets not having really got to know his rather enigmatic father, while Nicholas Reid is sorry that his father never met his wife or his children. But in other cases, the father's death – and, often, the mother's too – has some positive effect through freeing the son to regard his father openly and honestly, loosening his tongue and his emotions. Indeed, a fairly recent death is sometimes the catalyst for taking this step, as both Owen Marshall and Peter Russell acknowledge.

Most of the contributors, too, write predominantly with warmth rather than with resentment, anger, or hatred. This is understandable, given that it is probably more natural to want to conceal a bad relationship. The warmth arises out of a number of scenarios. Certainly, companionship, at some stage in the writer's life, is of real and lasting importance, whether in the context of sport (Murray Ball and Harry Ricketts), camping or walking (Owen Marshall and Greg Newbold), or simply sharing a house (Rupert Glover). Then there is the willingness of the father to defend the son in difficult situations or to give encouragement. Murray Ball's, Tony Simpson's and Greg Newbold's fathers all stand up for their sons, while Rupert Glover's is prepared to leave his son to his own devices on one memorable occasion. On the other hand, Denis Glover does provide continuing, if often tacit, support, as do most of the fathers, whether on the rugby field (Murray Ball) or in the world of books (Owen Marshall). In fact, to echo the title of Marshall's essay, books seem to be an important meeting place for father and son: several contributors recall their fathers reading to them or otherwise stimulating their love for literature.

Not that resentments are absent. These often stem from being deprived of companionship because the father has to work late (Greg Newbold), spends long periods overseas (Apirana Taylor), inhabits a world of his own (Owen Marshall), leaves the family (Tony Simpson and Philip Temple), is simply not interested (Chris Laidlaw), or is seemingly 'afraid' of his children (Bryan Gould). Strangely, perhaps, discipline has left few traces of resentment: most of the fathers either abdicate their responsibilities in this area (Rupert Glover and Peter Russell) or they are seen in retrospect as having dispensed punishment in a fair and reasonable manner (Murray Ball, Greg Newbold, and Nicholas Reid). An exception is Chris Laidlaw's father, who had a volatile temper. Also, in keeping with the New Zealand stereotype, many of the fathers tend to be inexpressive or shy away from emotion. Denis Glover, for instance, refused categorically to 'spew [his] guts out on anybody's coffee table'; Owen Marshall's, Peter Russell's, Chris Laidlaw's and Harry Ricketts' fathers seemed to want to deny the existence of feelings. And sometimes, as Russell shows, such denial can have a profoundly damaging impact on the son.

This has been only a fleeting analysis. Readers will discover more: that some of our fathers live cautious, conventional existences; that they have quiet disappointments; that they have problems with alcohol; that they have colourful love lives and secret inner lives; that they have embraced or rejected religion; that they are moral mentors or bad examples; that they have unusual or embarrassing habits, remarkable social skills and gifts for public speaking, or a charisma which both intrigues the sons and incites their envy. But whatever traits and experiences the fathers in this book have in common, and whatever is peculiar to them, they each had to come to terms, in their different ways, with what Owen Marshall refers to as the 'twitchy business' of life, and with having children – specifically, sons who would one day write about them.

Bill Sewell

DAD WAS MY SECRET WEAPON

MURRAY BALL on *NELSON BALL*

My father used to make me cry. One of my earliest memories is of sitting between his arms, astride the wooden seat he had made for me on the crossbar of his bicycle, with tears streaming down my face and my chest aching from the strain of crying. He is singing 'There's a Bridle Hanging on the Wall'. We are returning from whitebaiting, past the freezing works where he was a meat inspector. He, with a howling child between his arms, half a kerosene can of whitebait, and a net on his shoulders, and me, with a sore bottom and a heart overflowing with love for this man who was torturing me so – and for that poor, brave horse who had died in the flames to save his master. The anguish was exquisite. I used to plead with him to sing me that song – or the one about old Shep, the sheepdog who was also noble and dead. They were both equally effective in rendering me a blubbering wreck. And when we got home, Mum would cook us whitebait fritters for tea. Is there anything closer to happiness for a little boy?

I suppose today I would have been torn from my saddle (or 'Champion', as I believe I called it – after Gene Autry's horse) by a social worker or concerned citizen and my father charged with psychological abuse. Had anyone succeeded in prising me off my wooden saddle and away from my father, they would have been stalked for eternity by a vengeful, tear-stained little boy. They would not have escaped me for I loved my father dearly. I loved my mother, too. But Mum was not an All Black. It was not Mum who rescued me from the man next door in the strange affair of the unpainted letterbox.

We were living in Hastings at the time. Living next door to us was a little girl with whom I used to play. From time to time we had disagreements. The problem of the wet paint on the letterbox was one.

It had come into my head that her letterbox needed painting. This is unlike me. I am not good around the house, so the need must have been great. I picked up my imaginary pot of paint and my imaginary paintbrush and set about the job. My waving motions around her letterbox must have attracted her attention. She came out of the house and asked me what I was doing. A fair enough question, to which I replied politely and fully. And had that been the end of the matter, the whole nasty business would never have occurred.

But she, as many little girls are wont to do, butted in. She touched the letterbox to see if the paint was wet. Well, I could have told her the paint was wet. I was painting it, wasn't I? But she had to touch it with her finger. I pointed out that her finger had left a mark, and painted over the spot. Whereupon the little vandal touched it again – right where I had repaired her last dirty finger mark. This would have tried the patience of a saint, as it did mine, but I repainted it and warned her not to do it again. *She touched the same spot with the same finger again!* I put down my paint tin and brush, grabbed her finger and bit it. No man of spirit would have done less. She screamed and her father, who had apparently been watching us from the front room, came galloping down the drive to pull me off his daughter's finger.

He was in the process of shaking me loose and telling me what he did to mad kids who bit his daughter when my father arrived like the US Cavalry – or Gene Autry. Gene always arrived before the main rescue party and sorted things out. Dad, like Gene would have done, wanted to know what the trouble was. I explained about the painting job and my problem with the little girl who was ruining it. The man next door argued lamely that it was *his* letterbox and pointed out that it was still in its usual dilapidated and unpainted state, thus proving me a liar. And, to make matters worse, a violent, mad liar who attacked innocent children for putting their fingers on their own letterboxes!

My father, who was used to me and knew I did not tell lies because Gene Autry didn't, told him that anyone who touched his son would have to deal with him. There was a long pause. The man next door rocked back and forwards on his toes, getting redder and redder as he clenched and unclenched his fists. My father was not a big man – they made All Blacks smaller in those days – and the man next door seemed

MURRAY BALL,
JUNIOR ALL
BLACK, 1959

enormous. But I wasn't worried: I knew what he was thinking. He was thinking, 'This joker is an ex-All Black, I'd better watch my step here . . .' And he was right. I just wished he would try something. Gene was often smaller than the men he knocked down, too.

At last the man next door stopped pumping his face up. His hands fell to his side, and the purple colour trickled back to wherever it had come from. Taking his daughter's hand, he slunk back into the house, muttering darkly about what he would do next time and the need for lunatic asylums for kids. Dad and I were left masters of the field. I was sorry Dad had not knocked him down but felt that between us we had probably done enough to teach them not to mess with us Balls. I picked up my paint tin and brush and went home with Dad, leaving their letterbox partly finished. It is the last letterbox I have ever tried to paint.

To say that, as a little boy, I respected my father would be an understatement. I was in awe of him. Which is strange, because he was not really an awe-inspiring man. He was of about average height and weight, and had wrinkles that started with his tight, wavy hair and ran down his forehead to his eyebrows, giving him a slightly worried expression. I saw him many years later standing with a group of current All Blacks at a rugby reunion. He looked so small that you felt that any one of those giants could have carried him under an arm in a sprint without losing a yard of pace. But they would have had to deal with a pretty wriggly customer if he did not want to be carried. They might also have had a job catching him. Until late in life he retained a speed and agility that kept my brother and me well in our place as we grew into our adolescence. I remember, when the family was living in South Africa and I was a cocky First XV player, challenging him to race the length of the lawn. This was at a time when he was beginning to be plagued with arthritis. He shouted, 'Righto, go!' and shot past me in his grey slacks and leather-soled shoes like a grizzled whippet. He pulled up under the peach trees and waited for me to arrive. When I complained that I had not been ready, he beat me from a standing start in the race back.

Friends have told me how, as kids, they used to run away from their irate parents to escape punishment. My brother and I never ran away from Dad. One reason was that we were pretty sure he would have caught us. The other was that he had once told us that if there came a time when he could not catch us, we had better just keep on running. He'd said it with a smile but there was something in his voice that made us listen. Perhaps there was a third reason we never ran: it would have seemed cowardly and we did not want him to think us cowards.

Dad occasionally gave us a hiding. We almost invariably deserved it. I remember once when we were travelling in our heavily laden Commer van from Durban to Johannesburg. It is a long, hot, 640 km drive up from the coast to the High Veld. At this time, Dad was in the slot machine business and we had jukeboxes and pinball machines jammed from floor to ceiling in the back of the van. This meant my brother and I had to share the passenger seat with a pillow jammed in the gap between the two seats. I was about 11 and my brother probably eight or nine. The Commer was slow, and so heavily laden that Dad had to drive at top speed down the hills to get to the top of the next rise. It was hot, uncomfortable and boring for all of us.

My brother and I had been jostling and arguing for some distance, and Dad had asked us to sit still several times. Somehow Barry and I got into a fight over a comb. After a brief tussle the comb broke. My father did not say a word. He pulled over to the side of the road, got out of the car, vaulted a fence and broke a weeping willow stick off a tree. He climbed back over the fence, opened the passenger door and pulled us out.

There, beside the road, as motorists passed by, he whacked our bottoms with the stick. His method was to hold us by one arm and smack our rears with the other as we danced around him yelping. The blows often missed or were glancing but he landed enough solid ones for us to get the message. It settled us down and we did not charge him with assault at the police station in Mooi River, which was the next town we came to. I will not say he cured us of fighting for the rest of our lives, but his action did make the rest of the trip safe and tolerable. My father was right.

I guess this made us abused children. I can only wish that today's 'abused' children were as loved as we were.

When we emigrated to South Africa in 1948 – the year the Nationalist Government in South Africa came to power and began to institutionalise the policy of apartheid – the bonding of our family became more intense. Because we were strangers in a strange, and palpably hostile land, we grew closer. It was a strange sensation suddenly to be living in a society where social and racial groups actively loathed each other. The English-speaking South Africans hated and were hated by the Afrikaners, and both white groups hated, and feared the hatred of, the Blacks.

We were unaccustomed to the crude class system that permeated everyday life. My parents were unhappy, especially my mother. Mum had only agreed to go to South Africa for the five years my father expected he would need to make his fortune running gambling machines in partnership with my two uncles, who had become very rich in the business.

My elder sister returned to New Zealand to live with my grandmother. My brother and I were cast into school. Our arrival as aliens with funny accents coincided with the arrival of the 1949 All Blacks to South Africa. The team, under Fred Allen, proceeded to lose all four test matches. Had they known the torment their defeats were inflicting upon two little Kiwi kids at school among gloating South Africans, I am sure they would have found some way of winning a test or two. We sweated blood listening to the radio broadcasts. I remember straining every fibre in my body during those broadcasts, but it did no good. The All Blacks lost every test and went home, leaving Barry and me to face the music.

I had always intended to become an All Black. However, as we were living in South Africa – and I blush to admit it – I had half reconciled myself to playing for the Springboks. The 1949 tour changed all that. It became my obsession to return to New Zealand, get into the All Blacks, and come back to South Africa with them to wreak vengeance upon the entire South African people, especially my schoolmates. Dad was my secret weapon. He could show me how to do it. I don't know whether he knew of my plan, I don't remember ever telling him, but I was going to do it for him as well as for me. I knew he had suffered like us during that humiliating tour.

I also felt, vaguely but strongly, that he was not accorded the respect he deserved in this savage land. I think this feeling crystallised for me during the first test match between the Springboks and the British Lions in 1955. It was the largest crowd ever assembled for a rugby match. Dad, Barry and I had camped on the pavement to get tickets. And we, with the 95,000 other people, squeezed into Ellis Park on the big day. We stood on the bank – no seats and chest to back for five hours in the sweltering Johannesburg heat. During the third curtain-raiser, as the crowd creaked and swayed, I glimpsed Dad. He had been prised a little apart from me by the pressure of the crowd, and all I could see of him was his head. His chin was raised, as he strained to see over the buffalo shoulders of the giant Afrikaners in front of him. As I have mentioned, he was not a big man and at best he could have had only a partial view of the playing field. I looked across the stadium to the grandstand. High in its shady interior were rows of empty seats, waiting for the rich and privileged to arrive for the big game. I looked at the empty seats and then at my ex-All Black father battling in the heat to see the game he loved. That day, on the bank at Ellis Park, I became a socialist.

Dad worked hard. South Africa's National Government, as well as being deeply racist, were also deeply puritanical. They banned gambling machines, and the five years my father expected to need before he took Mum home to New Zealand extended to 10 and beyond. His pride would not allow him to go back to New Zealand before he was a wealthy man. His grandfather had been a barber in Foxton and Mum was from a family of landowners in the Manawatu. I did not understand it at the time, but his pride required that we return as wealthy as her family was.

So he worked. He was on call seven days a week to maintain his 'round' of pinball machines and jukeboxes. The telephone in our house was a death knell to family life. If we were going to the cinema (or 'bioscope', as we called it there) and the phone rang, the whole family would end up sitting outside some café while Dad in his khaki dustcoat laboured over a faulty wiring system or chewing gum in the slot. On a Sunday morning, before the family went to tennis, we might all be waiting in the car in one of Johannesburg's rougher suburbs while Dad grovelled in the back of a jukebox and 'ducktails' (local teddy boys) hung around making unfunny comments in their heavy accents. We hated it. It was boring and, also, we were snobs. We felt it was beneath our dignity

NELSON BALL, ALL BLACK

for Dad to be doing such work. But he kept going. 'When we get paid off' (that is, repay my uncle for the machines Dad had bought from him) became the phrase that stood between us and every luxury we demanded. I blush now to think of the way we nagged him. Mum was unhappy and eventually became very ill. And we boys did everything we could to avoid being pulled into the workshop to help him.

And we played rugby. As we progressed from team to team, Dad was there. He was always there. Every game, we thought he wouldn't make it. But every game, at the last minute, he'd be there. Often, just as we were lining up for the kick-off, we would spot him: a little figure high on the embankment, standing by himself. Behind him would be the old Commer van we thought ourselves too good for. He never missed. When it was over, he'd wait for us to get changed, have a word or two about our play and then go back to work.

That night he'd be home late after making up the time he had spent at the rugby. As he sat eating the over-cooked dinner that had been held for him in the oven, we used to talk about the game. Sometimes he would tell us about 'the great ones' like 'Cookie' (Bert Cooke) and Mark Nicholls, and how he felt rugby should be played – with daring and the boldness to run from anywhere. This was what he preached. We listened and believed.

The time came for me to return to New Zealand and get into the All Blacks to avenge the defeat of 1949. At the airport I said goodbye to my family. Mum was crying, Barry was silent and I think Dad was a bit choked up. I know I was scared. New Zealand had become a sort of Camelot in my mind. I had only hazy memories of the land and the people I was returning to. I had known ever since we arrived in South Africa that this moment would come. Now I suddenly realised I would be a stranger in my own country. I had a suitcase, a typewriter (which I did not know how to use), and a head full of half-formed memories of my grandmother and a cow called Peter. I also had a letter of introduction from my uncle to a rugby club he used to play for. Dad thought that his old club probably wouldn't remember him. It didn't seem very much to build a life on.

Dad was the last to say goodbye. He shook hands with me, his grip hard and just short of painful. He looked me in the eye, smiled his rare smile and said, 'Just do what you think is right.' His words plopped into the empty void that was my confidence and sat there like a wise old toad. I blame those words for much of my subsequent silly and irrational behaviour. But they gave me great comfort, and the old toad still sits, blinking its golden eyes, somewhere deep in my bowels. A precious and most needed gift.

I walked across the tarmac to the South African Airways plane with four propellers and a winged Springbok on its fuselage. My head was down and I watched the black puddle of shadow precede me. It slithered up the stairs ahead of me and disappeared along with Mum and Dad and Barry as I stepped inside. It was one day after my nineteenth birthday

Dad only saw me play twice after I left South Africa – in a minor rep game, where I pulled a thigh muscle, and an insignificant club game. He had built me but never ever really saw if I worked. I didn't get into the All Blacks in 1960 or any other year. I would have loved to have given him that.

Mum and Dad stayed on in South Africa. I made my home back in New Zealand. I visited them from time to time, and they came to New Zealand to see Barry and me. Our relationship remained strong, possibly because we were apart and appreciated seeing one another all the more. With separation came perspective. Dad became less my father and more an older man whose qualities I admired.

The 1981 Springbok tour of New Zealand split our family as it did many others. My brother and I were among the protesters; the rest of the family were supporters. My father was an old rugby man and accepted the pro-tour arguments that apartheid was politics and there should be no politics in sport. Barry and I, on the other hand, had seen apartheid and believed it should be fought with every available weapon. It was a painful deadlock.

I believe that Dad, if he had thought about it, would have considered himself a liberal – certainly in the context of the South African politics of the time. He always treated his Black staff well. (He now owned a large amusement park on the Durban Beach front.) Indeed, when the first cracks appeared in the apartheid edifice, he was in the forefront of those businesses which removed the signs reading 'NO DOGS OR BLACKS' from their entrances. This was well before it became legal to do so. But on the Springbok tour issue we remained at loggerheads. During the tour and up until his death, the subject was taboo. There was an unspoken rule that the subject should not be raised. It became like a piece of grit in an oyster. Eventually it developed a smooth surface and ceased to irritate.

Yet even during the full heat of the controversy, I never doubted Dad's love and support. I knew that if I needed him, he would be there. When I was not selected for the All Blacks in 1960 and returned to South Africa with my tail between my legs, he was there. When I had worked in England as a freelance cartoonist for more than a year without making any money to support my family, he was there. He bought us the cottage on Exmoor which allowed me to work. The money from the sale of this cottage enabled us to return to New Zealand, where I began work on *Footrot Flats*.

He thought I was mad and supported my madness unfailingly.

When he was dying in great pain of cancer in South Africa, he asked me to help him die. I said I could not. I fear it was cowardice on my part that meant I was not there the one time he needed me.

My father was not a great man. He was not even always a good man, but he was a great father. He gave me steadfast love and unfailing support. I believe it was these qualities of fatherhood that Jesus had in mind when he used the term 'Father' to explain his concept of God to his followers. Had I been among them, I would have understood.

WHO SAW CIPANGU

RUPERT GLOVER on *DENIS GLOVER*

The Cave Rock Hotel. Sitting on one end of the polished, horseshoe-shaped public bar. Too high to get down, even if I wanted to. Over my head the afternoon sun refracts through the amber liquid in the spirit nip glasses.

'A sarsaparilla for the boy, Denis?'

'Raspberry, Daddy.'

'Give him a raspberry, Frank.'

THE SUN PORCH at 10 Aranoni Track seems very long and elevated to a two-year-old. It commands a view spanning two-thirds of the compass, out over the scimitar of Pegasus Bay and west across the plains to the foothills and the alps of Canterbury.

The war is over but my father is back at sea, commanding a harbour defence motor launch of the RNZVR. The dull thud of the big guns from the batteries on Godley Head can be felt rather than really heard on Clifton Hill. Then, seemingly minutes later, without apparent connection, schizophrenically, a silent plume bursts from the sea as a six-inch shell smashes into the otherwise untroubled water.

'Is it a whale, Mummy?'

Just her and me, and the radio playing 'Whistle While You Work'.

MY PARENTS WERE both born in 1912, Denis James Matthews Glover in Dunedin, Mary Granville in Topsham, Devonshire. In 1933, at the age of 21, she emigrated to New Zealand. They were married in 1936 and honeymooned round the South Island in a baby Austin. When it lacked the power to mount hills, she got out and pushed while he stayed behind the wheel and slipped the clutch to keep it going.

In those last few pre-war years, life was good to them. The Spanish Civil War galvanised their political thinking. Denis founded the Caxton Press. Christchurch became the country's publishing centre and New Zealand literature came of age.

The outbreak of war changed everything. In 1941, Denis left for naval training in England and did not return for over three years, having served in the destroyer escorts on the Russian convoys to Murmansk and in the D-Day landings in Normandy. In 1944, Denis was granted home leave. Commissioned, courageous, decorated and unsettled, he had a girlfriend in London and a young wife in New Zealand. My mother, still childless, had joined the Women's Land Army and had spent the war years delivering milk in Christchurch. The two had been apart for more than a quarter of the eight or so years they had been married. He arrived in Christchurch in October, and shortly thereafter I was conceived – on the staircase in Mary's Papanui Road flat, he once told me.

Looking back, I believe their marriage may even then have been doomed. When asked by Customs whether he had anything to declare, Denis had replied, 'I declare I'm sorry to be back'. Restless and undisciplined in civilian life, he wrote letters back to England which show how hard he found readjustment to life in a small colonial town on the far side of the world. Certainly, my birth and the acquisition of a house on Aranoni Track – albeit accessible only on foot – gave him some real pleasure. His letters speak with pride of both events. And his constant preoccupation was still the Caxton Press. But trying to make a living as a jobbing printer, writing and publishing poetry, both his own and that of others, were not enough to still his restlessness. Increasing resort to the bottle led to deterioration, both personal and professional. By the middle of 1951 he had left my mother.

I LIKE PLAYING with the scissor-like fibre-needle sharpener that Daddy keeps with the wind-up gramophone. He puts on one 78 after another, Beethoven's symphonies or some other classical pieces which fill up a pile of records too heavy for me to lift. Mummy tells him not to make me sit and listen. I'll be bored, she thinks. But really I enjoy it. Not so much the music as the sharing of something with Daddy.

And sitting on the bathroom floor while he shaves. Today he's given me a tube of toothpaste, and I've eaten most of it before the inevitable happens. Mummy's cross with him but I'm feeling too sick to care.

But then he goes and I don't see him for days.

As I GREW older and went to school in Sumner, the days turned into weeks. Denis had moved to Redcliffs, a couple of miles round the road, where he lived on the estuary front with Khura Skelton, the woman who was to be his de facto wife for the next 20-odd years. She and her husband, Phil, had lived right next door to the Cave Rock Hotel in Sumner. Perhaps by design. Anyway, drinkers all, it was natural that my parents should visit them.

MESSING AROUND IN the garden outside the pub. Crossing the road to the beach. Back to the pub; 6:15. They'll be out soon. Then next door to the Skeltons'. 'One for the road, Denis'.

I CAN EASILY bike round to Redcliffs and see him. Sometimes I go to their house, but I don't like it much. I'm a bit scared of Khura, although to be fair, she never does anything to harm me. I just know somehow I'm not really welcome.

AT THAT TIME Khura was running a small shop on the corner of Wakatu Avenue and sometimes she would take time off and leave Denis in charge. I enjoyed visiting him then. There were always a few sweets handed out from the stock and he seemed cheerfully pleased to see me, more so than when he was at home with her.

One visit to the house was memorable, though.

I had seen a yellow sports shirt in the Sumner haberdashery. Covered with vulgar Hawaiian motifs, it was everything a small boy ever wanted. I looked at it in the window several times, then finally plucked up the courage to go in and enquire about the price, intending to save up my pocket money until I could afford it.

The shop was one of those old-fashioned places with a high counter the length of one wall and ceiling-high shelves behind filled with numerous white cardboard boxes. I think the other side of the shop had hangers and perhaps more shelving. Customers walked down the middle on a bare wooden floor which creaked in places.

I had got through the door and was halfway to the counter, where the haberdasher was standing writing something in an account book, when I heard the floor creak behind me. Two men in dark suits had come in after me. Before I had time to take stock of the situation, the shopkeeper greeted me.

'Ah, Rupert! Good boy! You've come in to pick up that package for your father.'

He reached under the counter and handed me a cardboard box just like all the others on the shelves behind him.

'Hurry away now and take that to Dad. He's waiting for it.'

I was totally bemused, but somehow had the presence of mind not to ask any questions. I left the shop immediately, slipping past the two men, and pedalled round to Redcliffs with the box.

Denis was home. I handed him the box and told him how I'd come by it. He opened it, and I could see it contained notebooks and papers but no clothing. He flicked quickly through the first couple of documents and burst into laughter.

'Good lad. Do you know what this is?'

'No,' said I, truthfully.

'This is Dick's book. He's a book-keeper who takes illegal bets on horses. Those men in the suits were detectives and you've just carried all the evidence of his activities out of the shop. He'll be grateful to you.'

I got my shirt, courtesy of the management. I expect he wrote it off on the books.

CHILDHOOD PASSED AS childhood does – very slowly when you're waiting for the holidays or a birthday, far too fast when those longed-for events finally arrive.

My father, having run out of options in Christchurch, moved north to Wellington. Now it was far harder to see him, particularly since I wasn't at all enthusiastic about going up there to stay. I was left in the care of my mother and, to his credit, I don't think Denis contemplated attempting to change that. Access was sensibly left up to me and, in those pre-teen years, I chose none.

All that is not to say that his departure had no effect on us. My mother's upbringing and background had not equipped her to make a living for herself as a solo mother in the New Zealand of the 1950s. The result of Denis' absence, combined with the almost blanket refusal of any of his lawyer friends – he knew them all – to pursue a serious main-tenance application against him, was that we lived in varying degrees of poverty which, at their worst, saw the power and the telephone cut off for want of means to pay the bills. I know now, looking back on it, that my mother occasionally went hungry to feed me.

We did visit Wellington once, I remember, staying in Khandallah with relatives of Rita Angus (who had lived just above us, on Aranoni Track). We didn't see Denis, but I remember being taken to meet my aunt, his sister Coreen, at the Wellington Railway Station. The steps at the front of that imposing building seemed huge to a small boy. And there, at the top of them, was Coreen. She looked at me and remarked, without a trace of humour, 'You poor little bugger. You've got the worst of both sides.'

FOR ALL THAT, it was a happy childhood. Sumner was a wonderful place to grow up in. Only 13 km from the city centre, it was, nevertheless, a different world: rural, maritime, self-contained. Sumner people, or at least Sumner children, didn't need the outside world. The school had a heterogeneous cross-section of pupils. I made lifelong friends and not a few enemies. The only child of a solo mother was an easy target and, without regular paternal tutoring in pugilism, I was on the receiving end of a fair amount of bullying from predators. Once, though, in January 1951, Denis got involved. We were at the Burgess Street house of some friends of his. All the parents were drinking. Some disagreement occurred between me and the son of the other family. We went inside to see if the grown-ups could sort it out.

'Fight it out like men,' said Denis. 'Go on, hit him!' Which the other boy promptly did, thereby settling the dispute in his favour once and for all. So much for my father's instruction in the manly arts.

Later that afternoon Denis, in expansive mood, climbed up onto an archway over a six-foot-gate and jumped off, breaking a leg in the process. Perhaps there is justice after all.

DURING THESE PRIMARY school years, I developed a passion for science, and in particular astronomy. Although it was commonly thought that I had a dazzling scientific career ahead of me, I see now that what had really got me in its grip was my own imagination. Science was a window to the universe which was far more exciting than fiction. While others were reading *Biggles*, I was devouring Fred Hoyle on the nature of the universe. While my friends were listening on their crystal sets to the one or two local radio stations on the air in those days, I was to be found

DENIS AND
RUPERT GLOVER

outside with a variety of optical aids charting the craters on the moon, the satellites of Jupiter, or the rings of Saturn.

My main contact with my father at this time was by mail. He always replied to my letters and encouraged my interest in star gazing. If he found a tome on astronomy in a second-hand bookshop in Wellington, he would send it to me.

At the age of about 12, I wrote my own definitive treatise on the origins and nature of the universe and posted him the finished product, resplendent in a hard-covered exercise book, with a note explaining its seminal importance to the future of astrophysics. I finished on a hopeful note: 'Are you going to print it?'

Rather than patronising me, he wrote back in a congratulatory vein and said he would see what could be done.

One day a large brown paper package addressed to me arrived in the post. Inside I found a hundred or so copies of my masterwork, *The Starry Void*, cleverly typeset and designed, with a note saying 'Well done'. I put them on sale at one shilling and threepence, thereby making, thanks to Denis, not a little undeserved pocket money.

That gesture was to be typical of his attitude to me for the rest of his life. No matter what hubris I showed, he was never anything but encouraging. I can see now that many of my enthusiasms were emulations of his achievements – Greek, sailing, the mountains, even writing poetry. This fact cannot have escaped him, but he never pointed it out to me.

The one thing he didn't seem to care for was my learning to play the violin. 'No son of mine plays the violin,' he said to Betty Wright on one of his visits to the South Island. Betty, the wife of Albion Wright, printer, advertising man, and sailor, was a policeman's daughter not given to understatement. She was quick to retort: 'Is that so, Denis? How do you think he feels about having a poet for a father?'

On that trip he recorded himself on Philip Wright's wax-cylinder Edison talking machine.

'Hello South Island. Hello South Island. This is Glover.'

I think Albion's gin bottle must have taken a punishing that day.

CHILDHOOD SLIPS NONE too gracefully into adolescence. The primary school pupil turns into the secondary school student. The ease of old friendships becomes the self-consciousness of new encounters. 'Girl' becomes the most alluring pejorative in the language.

Sumner suddenly stopped being the centre of the universe. My world expanded to embrace the Ministry of Works-designed co-educational complex that was Linwood High School. I disliked it from the day I arrived to the day I left, although I still think of one or two of my teachers with some affection and gratitude.

It was early on in these years that I started seeing Denis again. It was, perhaps, time to lay some ghosts. So, one high-school holidays, I plucked up enough courage to go north to visit him and Khura in Paekakariki. I managed to persuade my best friend, Simon Pascoe, nephew of Denis' old mountaineering friend, John Pascoe, to accompany me. Together we headed off into unknown seas north of Cook Strait.

As I recollect, we were well-received. A car (I think an aged Austin or Morris) was made available to us. We were allowed to drink beer and were generally treated as being a good deal more grown up than we really were. We met Fred Turnovsky's beautiful daughter and even accompanied her to a dance in 'Paraparam', as Paraparaumu was called in those days before political correctness. It was a confidence-builder. Denis and Khura weren't as intimidating as I'd feared. (That notion could have been fed by my poor mother's occasional threat to send me to live with my father when I got too poisonous to be handled in any other way, a prospect which had greater disciplinary value than the back of her hairbrush, which was also applied from time to time.)

Throughout my teenage years I returned to Paekakariki irregularly. I enjoyed it. Khura's frequent drunkenness was compensated for by Denis' good-natured treatment of me, regardless of the scenes she would create – and try to involve me in. For all that, I was ambivalent. Part of me resented him for leaving my mother to a hard life emotionally and financially. But he had only affectionate words for her, so I couldn't really take him to task even if I wanted to, which, mostly, I did not.

Besides, he was seductive for a young man keen on expanding his horizons. Charismatic, wherever he went he was welcomed and admired, or so it seemed to me. Once, a complete stranger left a group surrounding Denis in a pub near Buckle Street, came over to me and told me my father was a great man, a Prometheus unbound by the rules of others. He had a tear in his eye as he returned to buy Denis another drink.

That sort of comment was not unusual from both men and women. He had his detractors, certainly, but he seemed to inspire an uncritical loyalty and affection in a surprising number of people from all walks of life. I grew used to it, but it always made me vaguely uncomfortable, even when the praise was from people of prominence, household names. He seemed to know them all. Riding on his coat-tails, I could even get free beer at the Waikato Breweries in Hamilton. Heady stuff to an 18 year-old student in the days of 6 o'clock closing and a minimum drinking age of 21.

High school dissolved into university, university into my first real job. In 1969, armed with my freshly acquired MA (Denis had only a BA at that time – his LittD came later), I joined the New Zealand National Film Unit as a trainee filmmaker. It meant moving from Christchurch to Wellington: contact was now possible on a daily basis if I sought it.

PROXIMITY BROUGHT WITH it a measure of clarity, clarity about the destructiveness of his relationship with Khura and about the damage that their drinking was causing. Pride in his company turned imperceptibly to embarrassment on occasions when his drinking made him not interesting but grotesque. He always seemed to retain his sharp intelligence, but his body let him down. Unsteadiness became falls. Being his companion in public literally meant being, as often as not, his support.

There was a sense of desperation about their lives, the more poignant when he lost his last full-time job because of his propensity for repairing to the nearest pub at every tea or lunch break. Khura struggled on, with her own gin addiction, working, I think, in the Department of Agriculture, then coming home at night to drink herself into hostile insensibility with Denis.

It couldn't go on and it didn't: Khura succumbed. Ironically, I was in the South Island on a film job, staying with my mother in Sumner. The phone rang. It was Denis, to tell my mother that Khura had died that morning. I don't think he knew I was there.

HE WOULDN'T LET me go to the funeral, and others have reported with some bitterness that he deliberately told them the wrong time, so that they arrived after the event. In truth, he could never brook the display of emotion, or at least not his own. For a man so apparently public, he was intensely private. 'I will not spew my guts out on anybody's coffee table,' he once said.

For all their earlier outward antagonism, Khura's death knocked him. He fell ill and was hospitalised. When he came out, I took him to live with me at Worser Bay, on a strict regime of controlled drinking which, as best I could tell, he respected. He was good company, and grateful.

Back on his feet, he moved into a flat in Hataitai. The drinking intensified, but so did his creative output. Now quite resigned to being unemployable, he set about writing and publishing. This was the period of *To a Particular Woman*, a collection of love poems which surprised even his devotees. The story of this period and of his subsequent courtship of Lyn Cameron, whom he married, have been told elsewhere and are not a part of my experiences with him, largely because, yet again, he deliberately kept me at arm's length. Although I lived little over a kilometre away as the crow flew, he made it clear I was not to come to their wedding.

He had never married Khura, and resisted divorce from my mother. Albion Wright said it was so that Khura couldn't pressure him into it. And during the 20 years after the war, right up until 1967, he kept contact with his wartime sweetheart in London, telling her that Khura was only a carbon copy of her: 'Unhappily she is so like you that it breaks my heart, and I have told her so.' Now, contemplating remarriage, he must again have bridled at the idea that anyone close to him should be there, in case they, or perhaps he himself, should see his vulnerability.

SHORTLY AFTER THIS, our lives moved apart again. In early 1972 I left for a brief trip to Canada and London which turned into a seven-year odyssey which has nothing to do with this tale, except that once again, contact was confined to writing.

There were, however, two events in those years between 1972 and 1978 which did affect us both. On 4 April 1976, Denis' granddaughter, Pia, was born. He immediately dubbed her Pianissimo. In July of the same year, on my birthday, Mary died. She had never remarried and loved him to the end.

I came back to New Zealand, bringing Pia with me. Denis, not surprisingly, did not attend the funeral, but he did come to Christchurch before I returned to Canada. He was obviously very saddened by Mary's death and told me that she was the only woman he had ever loved. Perhaps it was true in a way – of that more later. I returned to Canada where I remained until, in 1978, tired of French Canadian separatism and wanting Pia to grow up in New Zealand, I came home for good.

Contact was, of course, renewed. I did a small amount of film work for South Pacific Television which took me to Wellington, where I was able to visit Denis and Lyn, by now living in Strathmore. 'I am the Laird o' Strathmore!' he had told me in a letter to Montreal.

Lyn – patient, gentle, loving, sad Lyn – was looking after him as if he were a handicapped child. His grog was rationed and I think that, secretly, he was grateful for that. Strong liquor, often not ameliorated by food, had taken its toll on his once-strong constitution and had desynchronised his biological clock so that he would stay up and work or talk loudly at hours when everyone else was, or wished to be, well and truly asleep.

Lyn long-sufferingly put up with these erratic hours, ministered to his bodily needs, took him out from time to time in taxis (often to the University Club, where he would sit at the bar drinking 'teeny-weeny' triple vodkas), and encouraged and shared in his creativity. Childless, although once before married, she saw him partly as husband and companion and partly, I think, as a child. She recognised his genius and told me she wanted to save him for New Zealand. She was of independent if not affluent means and was happy to spend her time with this unorthodox and difficult but still loveable man. He responded to this with outward shows of affection which, when younger and more independent, he would not have cared to display. Identifying with his love of the sea, Lyn found and bought a tiny house on the saw-toothed shore of Breaker Bay, outlooking upon Barrett Reef at the entrance to Wellington Harbour.

On my last visit to Strathmore, sometime in 1980 (by which time I had started legal studies at Canterbury University), Denis invited me to join him for lunch in the Oriental Bay home of Sir Owen and Lady Woodhouse. Sir Owen was then President of the Court of Appeal and had been a friend of Denis' since their wartime days in England, when Denis had led him, petrified, along the roof of a night train between London and Southampton with the aim of making toast in the engine firebox.

'He's now some sort of a judge,' said Denis disingenuously. 'When you become a lawyer you might need a friend at court.'

It was, I think, the last time I saw him. After lunch, Sir Owen saw us down to Oriental Bay where Denis took a taxi and Sir Owen, who was going into town, gave me a lift. He asked, perhaps with prescience, if Denis was all right and said: 'He's the salt of the earth. If I can ever do anything for him, you must tell me. He would never ask.'

Soon thereafter, Denis and Lyn were to move to Breaker Bay. On the day of the shift, mainly done by others, Denis insisted he could carry a box down the steps from the house to the driveway below. On the path he fell. The move was completed but over the next day or so his condition deteriorated and he was hospitalised.

No one told me, at least not until the last night of his life. At about 7 pm I was phoned by his old doctor friend Ian Prior.

'Your father is in Wellington hospital. I don't think he'll last the night.'

The last flight to Wellington had gone. There was nothing I could do. Next morning Ian rang again. My father had died in the early hours of the morning. His last words were: 'I am *not* a pussycat'.

PIA AND I went to Wellington to make the formal identification and help Lyn with the funeral arrangements. The police picked us up and took us to the hospital. After we had seen Denis, looking healthier in death than at the end of his life, the police took us home. 'He was a great man,' the constable told us. 'If you're ever in Wellington and want a lift somewhere, just ring us. We'd be happy to help a son of his.'

So it was over. Over without a denouement, although perhaps that came the day we scattered his ashes at the heads of Lyttelton Harbour, with a naval escort to pipe him into the deep he knew and loved. 'Smooth carpet for keels,' he called it.

OVER. OR SO I thought. For, unknown to me, there was to be a sequel.

In 1997, by way of an unforeseeable series of coincidences, I met his love from wartime London. I had always known of her existence but nothing more. He had never spoken of her. No one, not even Albion Wright, ever told me her name. In 1944 he left her, returning home to his first child, the Caxton Press.

But now she was in Christchurch. A Russian-Lithuanian Jew who grew up in Glasgow, at 85 Dvorinka Natasha Elkind was the age Denis would have been if he had lived. She did not hide the fact that he was the love of her life, and talking to her, I suddenly understood that she was the love of his, despite what he had said when my mother died. He left her to return to The Caxton Press and in doing so, he lost both. They wrote to each other for 20 years and he asked her to come to New Zealand, to him. She refused, but was so distressed that she cut off the correspondence. He wrote:

It was an hour of need, Oh
I know now it was meant to be,
But even so – me, I lacked attack
Even in bravado
When I found you crying in your own lack.

Meeting Doree Elkind made sense of many things before more felt than understood. Her intelligence and beauty were a match for Denis, perhaps the only one he ever encountered in a woman. But even then he could not face his feelings. In a letter, he wrote (in words which also feature in the poem 'In Memoriam: H. C. Stimson') :

Longing to love you, drawing some sorry strength
From your cajoling, what a fool I was. . . .

The story's old. Why should it trouble me
More than the hurts of childhood?
Who saw Cipangu, so they say,
Sickness ate into after.

He left her in the wrong way for the wrong reasons and was, I think, never whole again.

And once I met a woman
All in her heart's spring
But I was a headstrong fool –
Heedless of everything
       Sings Harry.

A STRANGER IN THE FAMILY

BRYAN GOULD on CHARLES GOULD

I hardly knew my father. The Second World War began in the year I was born. My father – a bank clerk – was exempt from conscription but decided (I suspect for reasons of social pressure rather than patriotic fervour) to volunteer. He was away from home for the duration of the war. When he returned in 1945, he was a stranger, an intruder in the tight little family unit my mother had successfully created. He remained an outsider, a state of affairs he did little to try to change.

The irony of his volunteering for war service was that he was found to be medically unfit for service overseas, and spent the war in New Zealand. He joined the Royal New Zealand Air Force and endured a less than satisfying five years at various bases in the North Island. My earliest memories of him preserve the sense of tension of those rare occasions when he managed to get home for the weekend.

It wasn't that my mother was unhappy to see him. My parents showed little affection towards each other in front of others, including the children, but according to the standards of the day, they were a loving couple. The tension arose because my father's weekend visits were often 'without leave'. His success in avoiding detection depended on being able to catch a railcar which passed through Hawera (where we lived) on a Sunday night. Because it was wartime, it was impossible to be sure that the railcar would run as promised and that it would stop at Hawera. As Sunday evening approached, so would my father become more nervous – to the point of being physically sick. It had been something to do with what my mother described as 'stomach nerves' which had disqualified him from overseas service.

My father spoke little about the war. The only enduring evidence we children had of his wartime years was a large lump of what he said was titanium from an aircraft propeller that he had somehow acquired during his time in the air force. For years afterwards, he would work on small pieces of the metal, shaping and polishing them and inlaying them with paua shell. He produced rings, bangles, tie pins, and napkin rings in profusion and of a very high quality.

As a young man, he had been regarded as artistic. He was the eldest child (with five younger sisters) of a rather unsuccessful North Island farmer, but his grandparents were Christchurch Goulds. His grandmother had been born Kate Ballantyne, of an equally well-known Christchurch family. Granny Gould, as she was known in the family, was a formidable woman who took a close interest in my father's education and development. It was her money that financed his school fees when he was sent from the family farm in Piopio to Christ's College in Christchurch, a school of which his great-grandfather, George Gould, had been a founder. He subsequently moved to King's College in Auckland, presumably because it was closer to home. When he left school, no question of his going to university seems to have arisen. This was, I imagine, less a comment on his academic record than a reflection of what was then the norm.

My mother told us that he had wanted to be an architect; my father, in line with his general reticence, never mentioned this. But he did have on his bookshelves (which were not extensive) a couple of textbooks on calligraphy. Even my mother didn't seem sure whether they were the product of a correspondence course or whether he had actually enrolled in some sort of art school as a young man.

In any event, Granny Gould had decided. She used her influence to get my father a job in the National Bank. It had proved to be, my mother assured us with the experience of the Great Depression and the war in mind, an excellent and secure job. My father made no comment, but never thought of changing his job and stayed until he retired at 60. He was a loyal and conscientious employee. He was never destined for the higher reaches of management, but in due course became a senior branch manager and retired with an excellent reputation.

As he grew older, the evidence of his artistic and creative bent diminished. He would occasionally draw something, and a fire screen and a wooden tray, which he had elaborately carved in the Maori style,

Bryan Gould

were part of our daily lives. But little attention was paid or value given to these artefacts.

When he returned home after the war, my father joined a family unit which he was to get to know for the first time. My parents had married in 1938 and I was born a year later. They had scarcely had time to adjust to the new pattern of life – a new marriage, a new town (my father was posted from Wellington to Hawera shortly after the wedding), a new house, a new baby – when the war intervened. My sister was born in 1940, and a no doubt long-planned baby brother arrived in 1945.

My father slipped back with relative ease into the family environment. He was not the sort of man who hankered for the freedom of life in the services, nor did he give any sign of resenting the constraints of marriage and parenthood. On the contrary, I think in retrospect that he welcomed the comfort and security of the family. For a man of his temperament, being sent away to boarding school at an early age must have been a penance. Certainly, he never threatened his own offspring with such a fate, despite heavy pressure from his mother for him to do so. He seemed to have enjoyed his bachelor years, but his war service was undoubtedly a painful experience.

Yet he made little attempt to re-establish himself as a major figure in the family. He was content to accept a marginal role in the little empire which my mother had created during his enforced absence. My mother conceded primacy to him in many respects, but in those areas which touched directly on the lives of the children, it was clear that my mother counted most. We children had a direct and centrally important relationship with our mother. We dealt with our father at one step removed, conducting most of our dealings with him – even our conversations – through the agency of our mother.

He was a constant physical presence, and was clearly an important factor in my mother's life. But he sought and spent no time alone with his children. We sometimes almost had the feeling that he was afraid of us or, at the very least, had no idea how to treat us. He was content to subcontract his direct parental responsibilities to my mother.

He revealed little of himself to us, apart from a general air of calm and wisdom and a somewhat sardonic sense of humour. As younger children, it never occurred to us that there might be more to him than met our childish eye.

Yet, as I have grown older, and particularly since his death 10 years ago, I have come to see that he was a more interesting person than we had given him credit for. Without overstating the point, he was a man born out of his time. I do not say that he would have made more of a mark, but he might have led a more satisfying life at a different time or in a different society.

He grew up and led his life in a rural-based society of hard-drinking, hard-swearing men. He succeeded pretty well in adapting to such a society. He was always reasonably popular (though never a social leader). He enjoyed a beer (though he liked best sitting quietly at home in his own armchair with a bottle of beer and the crossword). He was a keen and proficient sportsman. As a young man, he had been an excellent tennis and badminton player and in later life he played golf with great enjoyment. He was a passionate follower of rugby on the television, though it was a game he himself had never played with any distinction.

While these aspects of his personality were real enough, they did not tell his full story. He seemed to live an inner and private life whose worth and substance it was impossible to judge, simply because it was so far hidden beneath the surface. His way of adapting to the society he found himself in consisted, at least in part, of withdrawal – though probably not a conscious one.

Yet he was clearly an intelligent, thoughtful person with a retentive memory and a lively interest in the world around him. He read little and had no cultural life to speak of, but he knew a lot. His views, though largely conventional, were not quite what might have been expected. He voted National (as far as I know) all his life, but he was a republican and a New Zealand nationalist. He was impatient of the Old World and, perhaps because of his wartime experiences, looked to the USA to offer the way forward. He eagerly embraced new technology. He was strongly egalitarian in outlook. He was not, in other words, your usual conservative.

Even so, it must have come as quite a shock to him when I emerged as a leading Labour politician in Britain. He responded with the same slightly amused, almost mocking, detachment with which he had greeted my academic success. He willingly accepted the congratulations of friends and family as I won various scholarships and prizes, but whereas my mother was intensely involved in my early development and regarded it as her own personal achievement, my father seemed bemused, as though it were nothing to do with him.

I left home at 17 to go to university. I hardly saw him after that, except for during holidays. The closest I ever felt to him was when my mother died, three years before he did. I flew back from the UK for the funeral. He seemed not so much pleased to see me as genuinely in need of my support, and that of my brother and my sister. We had always thought of our parents' relationship as a rather low-key affair. He surprised us all by bursting into tears as my mother was farewelled.

Looking back now, I feel a sense of regret, or of several regrets. I regret that I did not have more of a father of substance in my life. I regret that he himself seems to have had so few expectations and ambitions and to have striven so little to achieve them. I regret that when he died in 1987, I was deeply involved in running Labour's general election campaign in Britain and could not get back to his funeral. But mostly, I regret that I did not know him better.

I am now convinced that there was more to know, and a greater possibility of a valuable relationship, than we ever realised. Over recent years, I have caught myself – in the mirror or on the television screen – suddenly looking like my father, at least in terms of mannerisms or expressions. When it first happened, I was disturbed, even displeased. But now, I am happy to acknowledge my father's part in my life and in me. I think about him more often. I think my brother and sister would agree that we feel now a greater sense of respect and affection for him than we have done at any other part of our lives.

DRIVING THROUGH LIFE WITH THE HANDBRAKE ON

CHRIS LAIDLAW on GEORGE LAIDLAW

My father is dead now, so he can't dispute any of this. But he probably wouldn't anyway because he never really disputed anything, particularly in his later years. It just wasn't in his nature to stir himself. That would have meant taking a risk and risks had long been eliminated from his life. Although he was in many respects a model of sobriety, restraint, and responsibility, and presided over a fairly happy household for the most part, my father made me angry – often. I still have that anger even though it is receding, inevitably, as time erodes the sharp edges of the emotions that it fashioned.

Dad developed an uncanny ability to avoid involvement. It was as if the lights had been switched off, the doors closed and the hatches battened down on life. Home was a bunker from which sorties would be carefully and conservatively embarked upon. The spending of money was, if not completely unavoidable, to be done with the utmost reserve.

I guess what I am saying is that my father drove through life with the handbrake permanently on and that this had a rather profound effect on me. It served to propel me away from him and to generate in me an unconscious determination to be noticed in direct proportion to his obvious determination to remain unseen, head below the parapet, out of the firing line of unseen marksmen waiting to pick him off.

I eventually gave up trying to get a reaction, any kind of reaction from him. It would have meant lifting other stones that covered our relationship, and neither of us wanted to face that prospect. And, in effect, we never did. Before he died, the slow victim of respiratory collapse, the best I was able to do was to tell him that I loved him, without having to add the unspoken premise that this was in spite of the distance between us and the absence of virtually any meeting of mind or spirit for more than 30 years.

When I look back, I find it hard to remember very much that we actually did together, father and son. I never had any real sense of him as a companion and I came to envy some of my friends years later when I realised just how substantial their relations were with their fathers, compared to mine; and how mutually reinforcing that relationship can be. It took me a surprisingly long time to work this out. Perhaps I knew but couldn't bring myself to admit it, as a kind of defence mechanism. At the time it seemed perfectly normal for him to do his thing, and for me to do mine.

I can certainly recall feelings of being rather hard done by at having to cycle several kilometres at night, as an 11 or 12 year-old, to and from the Dunedin Municipal Pool for swimming coaching sessions. My friends were all driven there and back, and once in a while I would be able to hitch a ride. Mostly, however, I would do it alone and it never occurred to me, nor presumably to Dad, that I was missing out. To be fair, for much of my adolescence we didn't own a car and I had no choice but to cycle or take the bus; but even when we did acquire a car, there was no question of my father setting out to take the children anywhere. The car was only used when my father had a personal objective and that was not up for argument.

Although one can never be really sure about such things, I suspect the fact that my father never really enjoyed much attention from his own father may have conditioned his behaviour towards me. My grandfather, Gordon Laidlaw, was a quiet, gentle, unassertive man, if the family folklore can be trusted. He had the misfortune, or bad judgement, to have married the female equivalent of Joseph Goebbels, a woman who ruled the entire family by sheer intimidatory dominance. Her arrival on the premises would herald the death of spontaneity, the close-down of conversation, and a sense of foreboding as to whom she would fix her attention on first. A cloak of Presbyterian probity would be thrown over the whole household and a loose word would be punished unmercifully.

When my father was a teenager, his dad was discarded. My grandmother had inherited some money and like a redundant employee, Gordon was handed a few bob and shown the door. Although the family never discussed the matter, it seems that she just got bored with him.

There was apparently no other competition. It wasn't a matter of being thrown over for somebody else with more charms. Gordon just didn't measure up any more. I remember once asking my father why his parents divorced. He said he didn't know and didn't want to talk about it anyway – it was a long time ago and wasn't important any more.

Interestingly, my grandmother shortly afterwards entered into a most unlikely relationship with a Scottish naval petty officer who happened to be visiting Dunedin and who threw over his career and stayed, later to marry her and take up where Gordon had so abjectly left off. They made an extraordinary match: she, a severe, puritan bully, and he, a rollicking old sea dog with a salty wit and a store of exotic stories, some of them involving maidens in faraway ports. He had a highly developed taste for the single malts that even my grandmother could not suppress.

The relationship between stepfather and son was not a very close one. I could of course only observe it much later, when they had learned to accept one another, but it must have been very difficult when old Jock, as he was called, first invaded the household. My father, even in later years, seemed to be slightly awkward in Jock's presence. He would retreat and let Jock dominate the attention of everyone present. The reality was, however, that the whole family – Jock, Dad, and Dad's younger brother Keith – were marshalled about like tin soldiers by the matriarch.

Dad's father Gordon was, effectively, written out of the script forever. I never heard my father refer to anything he and his father had ever done together and they very rarely saw each other, even though they were both living in the same city. In the early 1960s, after my parents had moved north to Wellington, I struck up something of a relationship with old Gordon. By this time he was effectively bedridden, and quietly declining with cheerfulness and stoic dignity. I was keen to find out what he was like and would sit at the side of his bed asking questions about the past. He revealed little and I began to believe that some grand cathartic event had erupted in the family long ago, leaving him as the chief casualty. If something like that had happened, I was never able to wring the facts out of either him or his son.

He told me that he and Dad had never had much of a chance to get to know one another. He was sad that things had turned out that way and he seemed to accept with a gentle fatalism that life had dealt him an unspectacular hand. I can recall feeling angry that he had been so

CHRIS LAIDLAW

severely frozen out by both his sons. I felt angry *at* him, too, for seemingly accepting that he deserved to be rejected. Perhaps he had.

The model was not a particularly propitious one and my father seemed to perpetuate it. He never seemed to be there when I had something special to do. He didn't come to Saturday morning sports or just about any other school activity that any of his children indulged in. Largely under pressure from my mother, he would turn out for events like the national swimming champs, in which I came within a whisker of winning New Zealand titles for a couple of years – thwarted only by the phenomenal Dave Gerrard. He would exhibit the mildest of enthusiasm and never, to my recollection, did I get a word of genuine encouragement, let alone congratulation. All that did was to raise my determination to do even better.

I do have one distinctive memory of a visit, alone with my father, to another town. For a time Dad was a travelling salesman for the large Dunedin drug company where he worked for all his life. Once, out of the blue, he decided to take me with him on a sales visit to Timaru in the company car, with an overnight stay at a local hotel. It was as far afield as I had ever been and I had never stayed in a hotel before. The hotel, the Grosvenor, was a rather grand establishment in those days, and it seemed to me – a wide-eyed nine year-old – to be a veritable palace: I can still vividly remember the gilt mirrors, the ornate staircase, and what seemed a wonderfully opulent dining-room. Perhaps the memory has stayed with me so clearly because it showed, once, that he genuinely cared about me – a memory too precious to let go.

There was one other thing we did together when I was around 10 or 11 years old: rabbit shooting. In those days, rabbits were everywhere around the Otago Peninsula and shooting expeditions were very popular, particularly if you could sell the meat to a local butcher. Dad was enormously enthusiastic about this. He had hunted rabbits ever since he was a boy and had become something of a crack shot with the old family .22. He would clean the rifle for days beforehand and count out the ammunition that he kept in a special drawer in his bedroom. He taught me how to shoot and where to position yourself to get the best shot. I loved every moment of it. It is difficult to remember how many times we went roaming the hills of the peninsula; perhaps a dozen or so. My first kill came after countless misses and I remember insisting we take the rabbit home and cook it. My mother, who disliked the whole concept of killing animals and certainly didn't appreciate the prospect of having to skin a rabbit before cooking it, objected, and the sad little creature was disposed of forthwith, my protests notwithstanding.

On those hunting expeditions, the gulf between me and my father was eliminated for a few exhilarating hours. But it didn't last. One day Dad announced that he had sold the .22. No particular reason: he had just had enough of rabbit shooting. Such was my enthusiasm, however, that I began to go out shooting with a friend and his father; then later, when we were old enough, with just my friend. The disappointment of not going with my father didn't last long.

As far as I can recall, apart from the occasional holiday at Karitane Beach in my early teenage years and the odd night at the speedway in Dunedin, we never spent any more real time together. He was into bowls and gardening and that was that.

By the time I had reached 14 or 15, I was more or less a free agent. Family holidays were replaced with peer group adventures as far away from the family circle as possible. Our paths didn't really cross again until many years later, when both parents came to stay with my wife and me in Paris. In between lies a void, an absence of any communication beyond the most rudimentary kind. He was uninterested in what I was doing and vice versa.

My father's most frustrating preoccupation – it seemed to me as well as to both my sisters – was the elimination of all opportunities to indulge in extravagance. This meant that lights left on, baths overfilled, and food not finished were all punishable offences, and punishment was invariably exacted. My father had a very volatile temper if his authority ever appeared to be under challenge, and there were moments when it boiled over into violent reprisals at the seemingly mildest of offences.

One such instance, seared into my psyche for life, was provoked by a haircut. Dad, whether to save money or to ensure that the final product was to his conservative liking – probably both – insisted on always cutting my hair himself. He had a pair of none-too-sharp scissors, an ancient comb, and one of those hand-operated pairs of clippers that pulls out as much hair as it cuts. He was convinced of his infallibility as a barber in spite of the patently disastrous results. I would emerge from these ordeals with a bizarre crop of misshapen hair on top, surrounded by tracts of semi-baldness. These haircuts were tests of endurance as well, since my father would not tolerate the slightest bodily movement which, given the quality of his equipment, was in any case highly inadvisable.

On the occasion in question, my older sister, who derived sadistic pleasure from winding up my father's temper so long as I was the victim, concealed herself behind a sofa from everyone else except me and began to pull excruciating faces while I underwent the ritual of the haircut. The result, no matter how hard I tried, was the slow build-up to a dam-burst of mirth, and the result of that was a slip of the clippers, an explosion of anger from my father, and a severe hiding with a leather belt.

I was not often beaten by Dad. It only happened when his temper got the better of him. The merits of the case for discipline had very little to do with it. As the only boy around the house, I became a natural target. My sisters had a knack of being able to melt away whenever trouble loomed. I would stand out all the more. It seemed very unfair to me at the time. I rarely got away with anything, and every once in a while my mother, who was afraid of my father's temper, would try to divert his anger away from me.

By the age of 12 I was a fanatically keen rugby player. I particularly prided myself on my goalkicking ability and had a special training routine that involved placing the ball on the front lawn facing the house, then kicking it directly over the large, central brick chimney at the top of the roofline, and landing it on a compost heap in the back garden. I could drop it there on average four times out of five. One day, after a heavy shower of rain, I teed up the ball and advanced upon it, Don Clarke-style. Alas, the wet grass intervened – I slipped as I kicked and the ball, instead of soaring over the roof, cut a trajectory straight through one of the large Victorian sash windows that were the main feature of the house and for which it was more or less impossible to find sufficiently large replacement panes. The awful implications of an offence of this magnitude were lost neither on me nor my mother. She was aghast at the likely outcome if it were revealed that my goalkicking, which was not approved of by my father in any case, had been the cause of such profound devastation.

Heroically, Mother herself claimed responsibility. It was the broom handle, she said. Apart from a lengthy lecture about clumsiness, there was no other retribution. After all, damage that had resulted from honest housework, rather than from idle sport, was less punishable. She got away with it, and so did I – a rare victory.

My mother was perpetually intimidated by Dad. Like so many other women of her generation, she had few rights, no personal income of her own, and no power over the disposition of family resources. When we eventually got a car, Dad would not let her drive it. Much later, when my parents moved to Wellington, she actually bought her own car, but my father began to drive that as well and eventually finished up more or less taking it over. Her frustration was, of course, subliminal. I was vaguely aware of it, as were my sisters, but we had no alternative frame of reference to use as a basis for objection. My mother therefore bore her burden with stoicism. Compared to many other women she was, after all, fairly lucky.

By accepting this situation, my mother was never able to exploit her many personal talents. Everything revolved around my father's preferences. After he died, Mother began to realise how angry she had become over the years at having no choices and in the end very little of a private life. In a curious way, that frustration at not being able to assert herself as an individual was compounded by her constant identification as the 'mother of an All Black' rather than as a person in her own right.

My personal success in the outside world, first in sport, then later in public life, became a source of difficulty in my relations with both parents. My father could never quite bring himself to acknowledge it openly, having never enjoyed any great feeling of success himself. From a very early stage I knew instinctively that he felt personally diminished by it. Was this normal? I can remember other parents parading their children's successes with justifiable pride, but never once did I hear my father sing my praises. The absence of parental reinforcement, more than anything else, drove a wedge between us that was never removed.

Of course, my father was a product of the opportunity-starved Depression years and there was a certain amount of generational contrast in circumstances. He would comment on how much easier everything was for the baby-boomer generation, how difficult it had been to make ends meet in the 1930s: the sort of stuff that a sixties kid had no time for but so many parents traded on. The problem was, my father used this as an excuse.

For a long time, much too long, I convinced myself almost unconsciously that I should compensate for my circumstances – a handsome salary, life in a series of exotic cities, and a lifestyle that my parents could scarcely imagine – by giving them expensive gifts. Needless to say, this was not a very subtle response because both parents were locked into a mind-set that regarded any exhibition of material wealth as next to sacrilege. It began to dawn on me, very late in the piece, when I returned from a diplomatic posting in Zimbabwe in the late 1980s, that I had been carrying this sense of guilt about affluence all my adult life, largely because of my father's denial of the positive virtues of having money – and spending it.

Dad could never bring himself to face his inability to deal with money, to regard it as a form of energy and abundance rather than a source of anxiety and trouble. He kept his savings locked firmly away in the Post Office, in an account earning several percentage points lower than the lowest bank deposit rates. Whenever I broached the subject of making his money work a little harder, by investing in commercial bills or even in the share market, the response was always the same. He was convinced that all banks were crooked or at best unstable and, after waiting years for something to back up his claim, pointed gleefully to the near-demise of the Bank of New Zealand in the late 1980s as clear evidence of the incompetence of bankers. All such institutions could not be trusted. The prospect of placing his own personal nest egg in the hands of the get-rich-quick brigade was something he would not even allow himself to contemplate. He hated property speculators, and his whole being was affronted by the thought that someone could make money by taking risks. There was something ineffably unfair about money begetting money.

And so, inevitably, my father's nest egg never increased in size. He would never reveal how much he had stashed away at 3 percent or less, and he would skilfully divert the conversation if ever asked. My mother had no idea either until after he was dead. He steadfastly battened down the hatches in his declining years, eliminating all but the most unavoidable expenditure, proud of owing nobody anything, paying his bills with cash ('real money') and eschewing such fripperies as cheque books or credit cards. For Dad it was life in the slow lane, where he felt comfortable and not obliged to anybody.

My mother knew this minimalist approach to life was silly but bought into it out of loyalty, to the point where she must now be actively persuaded to spend money, to derive some enjoyment from it in a way my father couldn't. Alas, all genes will have their way, in spite of our best efforts to deny them, and I recognise some of this negativity towards money in myself. At least I can now see this for what it is and recognise the importance of extricating myself from it. For me it is a case of 'A luta continua' [The struggle continues]. It may take some time.

My father's minimalist approach is best illustrated by his attitude towards that most quintessential symbol of personality – the car. For much of my childhood, Dad managed to avoid the reality that modern families cannot function well in the suburbs without motorised transport. He would proclaim that he had taken the bus for 40 years and everybody else could do the same. Occasionally, on a Sunday, he would be granted the use of his mother's car to take the family out for a ritual excursion. These were ordeals of anxiety and tension. The horror of possibly having to explain away some damage, no matter how inconsequential, to the pristine Vauxhall Velox imposed a gigantic damper on proceedings. The temptation to travel at anything like the legal maximum speed was stoutly resisted. Ice cream or any other potentially messy substance was banned from the vehicle, and we children would sit rigidly at attention in the back seat waiting for permission to wind down a window and extend a tentative arm into what little wind was generated by the stately progress of my father's driving. None of us looked forward to these outings, still less when my grandmother herself decided to lead the expedition.

When, with the decline of public transport in Dunedin, it became virtually impossible to manage without a car, Dad lashed out on an ageing Morris Minor. Needless to say, nobody got to drive it except him. I took driving lessons from a family friend and as soon as I obtained my licence, announced that I was ready to drive the family car. Perhaps in order to ward off that prospect, Dad arrived home one evening, to my astonishment, with a European 50cc moped which he said was all mine. This was a big step forward for me. I was 15 and ready for the road in every sense. I sold the moped shortly afterwards and began a long love affair with motorcycles – the real kind – graduating from 125cc all the way up to a 650cc Norton Dominator, bought with the money I'd earned working in the school holidays at freezing works and wool stores.

Eventually I moved on from motorbikes to cars and by the age of 18 had a rather dignified Singer saloon. It was so dignified that my father took a particular liking to it. Whether he persuaded me or I persuaded him, I can no longer recall, but we finished up swapping cars and I acquired the Morris Minor. Dad pampered the Singer for another decade while I changed cars virtually every year, a practice he regarded as irresponsibly extravagant. When the Singer finally succumbed to the ravages of rust, he bought another relic of the once great British motor industry, a car that survives to this day as a rolling monument to his intense dislike for the new and the flash.

My family was almost completely non-sporting. Neither parent had come from sporting backgrounds and my two sisters showed little or no interest in sports. My parents and the wider family were therefore surprised when I threw myself into almost everything going at the time – swimming, water polo, basketball, cricket, gymnastics, surf lifesaving, a little golf, and, above all, rugby. By the time I was about 16 I was a nationally rated swimmer, a provincial rep in basketball, water polo and surfing, and a leading prospect in rugby. All this activity was conducted in an extra-familial context. My mother would occasionally come to watch and was always very supportive, but my natural instinct was to leave the family out of all this. Somehow it was my world, not theirs, and my father certainly never intruded. Unlike most families, we never discussed the race or the game coming up at the weekend, nor the tactics, the training, the dramas, and the disappointments.

By the time I left school, rugby and getting a good degree had become the driving forces in my life. I never discussed ambitions with either of my parents. There never seemed to be the time. Nor was there any real motivation on either side. I was totally independent and when my parents moved north to Wellington at the end of my first year at Otago University, I can remember a huge sense of relief. Now I could get on with the serious business of being a student free of interruptions.

If Dad was pleased at my academic and sporting progress, he was never able to say so. He did seem to be genuinely happy when I became an All Black at 19, but there was little by way of celebration. It was business as usual: no fuss, no emotion.

A year or two after that, Dad retired from the drug company, retreated to the Wairarapa, took up bowls and serious gardening, and thought of little else thereafter. I was increasingly out of New Zealand from this time onward and our encounters were confined to a day or two every couple of years, when I would come back on fleeting home leave visits. As time went by, he became more difficult to reach. We would often part having disagreed on almost every subject. I suspect that as often as not he deliberately set out to be contrary, to take the opposite view, no matter how illogical it might have been. I found these moments very dispiriting, particularly when he would debunk some of the principles I believed in passionately – and, I have to admit, inflexibly. At such times he always seemed to be mild-mannered and relaxed. If he found himself cornered in an argument, he would kill it off by resort to inanities like 'well, it'll all be the same in 50 years' or 'what goes round comes round'. Arguing with him was like punching at shadows.

Without ever seeming aware of it, he could also really hurt me. A year or two after Rob Muldoon had, under parliamentary privilege and fired up with alcohol, pronounced me a traitor for actively opposing him on the South African question, my father, in idle conversation, remarked that he admired Muldoon: 'Good bloke. Knows how to get things done. Doesn't take any nonsense from anyone. Best prime minister we've had,' was the general drift. I don't know whether he had personally felt any sense of injustice when he learned of Muldoon's attack on me; the pity of it is, I never asked him.

I guess that in the end Dad was in his space and I was in mine, and we both preferred it that way. When it became obvious, in 1995, that he didn't have long to live, I began to face the difficult realisation that there wasn't much time left to make my peace with him. After some excruciatingly awkward moments I finally found the means to tell him that I loved him – and as I said it, I knew that the sentiment was real. He seemed genuinely moved for the first and only time in my recollection. It wasn't a cathartic moment but it was the best that either of us could manage. And it helped.

When Dad died shortly afterward, my sense of loss was over what might have been rather than what actually had been. The one thing I determined on the day of his funeral was that I must never allow history to repeat itself. I suspect that even Dad would not forgive me if I did.

MEETING IN THE WORLD OF BOOKS

OWEN MARSHALL on *ALAN OSMOND JONES*

Was that me stealing coins from my father's trousers in the wardrobe? Trousers hung right way up from the braces, I think, rather than being folded over hangers, because I would put my hands stealthily and deeply into the pockets, all the while with an ear out for any sound of approach. The smell of his clothes then is present in my own wardrobe now, and I still experience the same emotions of familiarity and guilt and love. A shilling even was a sum which could corrupt me: it would give entry to the matinee at the bug house, or the town baths with hokey pokey as well to be chewed between honey-potting and lying on the hot concrete.

Was that my mild shame and contempt when at a mass picnic he leapt into a river pool holding his nose? Were those my observations of his harmless deceits? He had neither the inclination, nor the resources, for many good clothes and if caught out in an afternoon by an unexpected caller at the front door, would slip out of the back one, catch up the hoe, and come whistling round the house as a gardener to explain his collarless shirt and knee-baggy trousers.

Was that me who would come quietly into his study and run a hand along shelf after shelf of books to feel the changing textures and the corrugations of the spines; who would rustle the tissue paper that protected the illustrations in some Victorian editions, become aware of the smell unique to that room, watch him using his gold-banded, blue fountain pen?

Was that me in my father's church setting the little communion glasses in the holes of the polished, wooden carrier and swigging the

53

elderberry wine, while the colours from the stained glass windows played bruises over my skin and the organ-pipes rose as columns high into the arched ceiling?

In writing of my father and our relationship, I've no rigorous regard for factual accuracy. This is partly laziness, but more a belief that memory is often true to the dynamic influence of experience even when fact, or the opinion of others, contradicts it. Relationships are personal after all, no matter how many friends, or brothers and sisters, are in the cast. And many of the contradictions are simply evidence of the complexity of human nature. I'm aware also that I've been a very incomplete observer of my father's life, both through self-absorption and accidents of time and place. I have very few recollections before the age of five, and I left home for university at 18. The close relationship of childhood was replaced first by the fierce self-centredness of adolescence, and finally the irregular contact of an adult son with an ageing father. The image of my father is a composite one, but dominated by my youthful view of him between the ages of about 33 and 50. Most of his life, I now realise, hasn't been open to my scrutiny.

We never quite forgive our parents for treating us like children. When we lived in Blenheim in the early fifties, my grandfather Jones visited us occasionally, and I observed my father's affectionate mockery of him when his back was turned. I have indulged in the same sort of mockery of Dad with my brothers and sisters, and now I detect a furtive amusement between my own daughters of which I am the butt. We all play character parts in the end.

Alan Osmond Jones was born in New Zealand in 1909, shortly after his non-farming parents came out from England to the shock of an uncleared bush block in the remote Wekaweka valley of the Hokianga. Geographical isolation and poverty gave the family a pioneer experience typical of an earlier New Zealand. They built a two-roomed shanty home of totara, kahikatea and taraire from their own land. Dad liked to recall its split plank floor covered with sacks and rag mats, the camp oven and corrugated iron chimney, the calico rather than glass windows, the walls papered with the *Auckland Weekly News* and *Yates' Gardening Calendar* from which he learnt to read. At night he would lie with his brothers and listen to the moreporks and the kiwis in the bush which grew almost to the back door.

The few books brought from England – *The Pilgrim's Progress, The*

OWEN MARSHALL

Swiss Family Robinson, and Morley's *Life of Gladstone* among them – were treasured and much read by all in the family. The mail-order purchase of a new book was a great event, and Dad told stories of reading on horseback as he rode back up the bush valley after taking delivery at the distant store/post office.

The steep, rocky farm was rarely an economic proposition in the best of times and quite unable to provide for a large family in the difficult years. As soon as possible the sons and daughters had to seek work outside the district. Several of them worked on the roads, my father included for a time. Most of them became farmers, or farmers' wives. Grandfather Edwin Jones, from Middlesbrough, but of Welsh descent, did his best, but was at times bewildered by the new life. Dad said he exclaimed vehemently that 'the guts of my pigs don't come out like the guts of other men's pigs'. My father's broad palms and heavy forearms remained a testimony to the slog of an early bush farm and wage labouring. He was of average height, though age reduced that in the end, and his legs were somewhat short in comparison with his arms and broad chest.

Dad was proudly Methodist. Ever since the days of John Wesley, his mother's side of the family had had a preacher in every generation. John Unthank, a farmer and local preacher in 1761, was my great-great-great-great-grandfather. Dad was the first ordained minister in this long line of preachers, and to his quiet delight my brother Barry followed him into the Church. Dad's formal learning never went beyond the three-day-a-week primary school, but by natural intelligence, determination, and self-education, he became first a home missionary then an ordained minister. At 19 he was riding horseback around the scattered Hokianga settlements to preach. Later he had an Indian motorbike, and there is a photo of him astride it, wearing a soft leather helmet.

Dad married Jane Marshall in 1935. The Marshalls have a connection with New Zealand going back to the 1840s and were a well-known pioneer farming family in the Feilding area. My mother's people came originally from Warwickshire, where they farmed at Halford Bridge, near Stratford on Avon. In 1996 my wife and I visited the lovely part-Norman church there and took photographs of old Marshall graves. We had a drink in the local pub, which may well have been more popular than the church with the original Marshalls.

Dad and my mother had three boys – Hugh, Barry and myself – but Mum died of breast cancer in 1944 when she was only 33 and I two-and-a-half. Dad never spoke of our loss to me, but after his death in 1995, I read his diary entries of the time and was moved, although not surprised, by the demonstration of his faith. On the night of her death he wrote, 'I am still much stunned by news, but God will bear me through. I who have tried to point others to him in such times must now myself turn to him. He will not fail. My dear girl trusted in him and that is to me a tremendous joy.'

After the death of my mother I was looked after by a kindly aunt as part of her own family, and returned home shortly before I was five. Not long afterwards Dad married Violet Kruse, a deaconess in the Methodist Church, and in time they had six children. All of us got on happily enough, though the elder ones had moved on before the younger ones could get to know them.

Children take their own situation as the norm, and I rarely considered what impact the loss of my birth mother may have had on me. More recently I've wondered if it explains the coolness and self-sufficiency – selfishness another reading – of my nature, and the dominant influence my father had on me as a child.

Because of the time spent away from the family after Mum's death, my first clear recollection of Dad is from the comparatively late age of five when we were living in Wanganui. I returned from school to find him in bed with jaundice. His yellowness was the reason the memory was imprinted, but I remember as well the sense of security and good-will I almost always had in his presence. From about the same time I recall lying in the darkness of my bed, needing to go to the lavatory, but terrified by Dad's snoring, thinking it the menacing growl of a bear in the passage, and finally wetting the sheets rather than risk a mauling.

My father had an indomitable Christian faith, but I remember him even more as a man of reason: a just man, a man to be influenced by sound, fair argument rather than emotion and self-interest. He was a cool man; cool even to those closest to him, cooler to those outside the family, though sincere and caring in pastoral work. As far as I remember, he had no close friends, no regular cronies for a boys' night out. His occupation, his interests, and his temperament set him apart from most of society, I imagine. He was respected, often admired within the limited community known to him, but he was not a man of familiarity or easy conviviality. His nature was an interesting amalgam that came from an early, almost pioneer rural experience, a self-educated bookishness, and the provincial life of a circuit minister. It seems to me that the people of my own generation have often had a more general and predictable development than that of the generation before.

He was never, never a petty man and in that so different from many of his fellows. Pettiness and triviality and envy were things I had to learn outside the family. He was never interested in the snide gossip of the neighbourhood, or the confining nature of friendships compounded partly of competitiveness, partly of need and affection, partly of jealousy and curiosity.

Dad never shouted, never lost control in my presence, never indulged his own mood at the expense of others and rarely complained of any hardship or disappointment. Very occasionally I saw him angry, and always with good cause, but anger made his voice quieter, his actions both more deliberate and determined. He struck me with a fruit tree switch or the razor-strop for the more serious offences of theft or insolence, but then as now, I was able to see the justice of it and the motivation of duty. Malice and cruelty, I truly believe, were known to him only through the actions of others.

My father was completely lacking in any public conceit or any urge to establish precedence, or status, for himself. He considered himself the equal of any man, and any man quite likely to be his equal. It was the worth of a person's essential character and achievement that impressed, or dismayed, him and he was never awed by trappings. The hype and sensationalism, the shallow celebrities and media-received views that increasingly dominate life were objectionable to him.

An illustration of this side of his nature occurred in the early 1950s when the Queen visited Blenheim. Along with other people of note in the town, he was invited to have a seat on the stage built in the open town centre from which the Queen would speak. I imagine that he was mildly interested to take part: he always looked to Britain as the source of our culture. But what I remember so clearly is the unstudied calmness with which he regarded the event. Our house on High Street was on the route the royals and their entourage were to take to the square, and long before the time set down, the footpaths were crowded with excited people. My father worked in his room until a few minutes before the time appointed, then walked quietly down the street and took his place amongst the small-town dignitaries. I have no recollection of how he afterwards described the event.

Virtues often have their flip sides, and it was so with Dad. Sometimes his rational principles were exercised with too little regard for circumstance. I remember in form one the humiliation of being unable to pay the 'fees' that Marlborough College imposed, because Dad upheld the statute establishing education as free, compulsory, and secular. I also remember my stepmother finally and secretly giving me the money from her very shallow purse. Better, I think, if Dad had approached the school directly rather than using an 11-year-old son as an intermediary for his protest.

At the end of my fifth form year in Timaru, Dad told me that I would have to leave school and get a job, because my two elder brothers had done so by the same stage, and for me to receive more years of secondary schooling would be unfair. My brothers were happy for me to continue, but I was allowed to do so only after agreeing to pay some board, which I obtained from an after-school job, and provide some of my own school clothes. We had an argument as to whether my child allowance should be taken as part of my board payment. Even then I saw the irony of paying to be at school, amongst all those reluctant comrades. Dad must have been very aware of the demands of a large and growing family on his limited stipend, but for a lover of learning and literature it was an odd stance to take.

Like many who lived through the Great Depression, my father was very close with his money, but in him frugality – at times, stinginess – remained strong throughout his life. With his younger children he was able to be more generous than during the years I best recall. He was always on the lookout to make economies, and they provided us with rueful amusement behind his back. He would walk through the house in the evenings turning out lights; he questioned the monthly grocery bill item by item; he seized stray pieces of wood for the fire while about his daily business; at one stage he instituted a weekly butter ration for each of us; he ground acorns and had my stepmother make unpalatable muffins from the flour; he cut our hair and resoled our shoes with equal incompetence; he had an encyclopaedic knowledge of, and extra pastoral concern for, all the homes within his circuit at which he would be welcomed with a scone and a cup of tea. My brother Hugh delights to tell of hearing him admonish my stepmother when she decided on the glaring luxury of ice cream for dessert. 'Don't put it out, Vi,' he said. 'They'll only eat it.'

When we lived in Blenheim, a generous farmer from the congregation contributed a cow to our household. It was grazed on the outskirts of the town and my elder brothers each took their turn at pedalling out before school and milking it. At about age 11, I inherited the job. After a short time the arrangement was changed, perhaps because I was not such a skilled milker: the cow was returned to the farmer and each day I had to bike over 5 kilometres to the farm at milking time and then back with a billy of charity. It was a chore I disliked. At first the novelty was such that I persuaded a friend or two to go with me, but they soon recognised the task for what it was and preferred to stay in bed a little longer. Dad would let the milk settle in a stainless steel bowl, then skim off the cream and often make his own butter by shaking it in a preserving jar.

While still at primary school, I climbed Mount Riley with Dad and my brother, Barry. Just a Marlborough hill, no doubt, and I've never returned to witness its diminishment, but I remember keenly the sense of disappointment when Dad reneged on his reckless promise at the summit to buy fish and chips for tea, after customary budgetary caution returned at lower altitude. During my boyhood we never ate in a restaurant, never went to a stage show, and Christmas presents were oranges, a pair of pyjamas, books rather than the pedal car of our dreams. When adolescence came, it seemed that I would be eternally in short pants because of the expense of long ones, and it was finally Hugh who bought me a pair from his own earnings.

There was no harm in all of that, and no hypocrisy either. Dad spent least on himself. He didn't drink, smoke or gamble, wasn't interested in clothes, had no even moderately expensive recreations. This makes him seem a narrow, crabbed man, but he wasn't. He was surprisingly tolerant, open-minded, intellectually curious and happy in the natural world.

Although he was not a sophisticated man, my father's intelligence, his power of concentration and expression, his lack of a disabling cynicism, and his steadfast faith, made him an interesting man and, in his own modest way, an impressive one. Essentially his life was of the mind, and sometimes that meant a lack of priority and concern for other people – even his own family – which amounted to selfishness. He would recite lines of poetry or smile to himself at something recalled from his reading, or past experience, while with other people. There were very few people whose company was preferable to his books. Often he would go through several of the Welsh names of his children before striking that which was applicable to the one before him: 'Ah, Barry, Owen, Lloyd, Evan . . .' Before he took me to enrol at Timaru Boys' High School, the Rector of which was fellow Methodist Mervyn Bull, he had not talked with me about any course subjects and was unaware of my marks from primary school. To me at least, he was a very poor correspondent, and after I left home I had the feeling at times that it was out of sight, out of mind; but the fault was no doubt equally mine, for once fledged I seldom returned or saw a need to keep in touch. Individualism was very much the thing in our family.

But to put against any such neglect in practical matters were the times he read to me from Coleridge in his study, told me of Gladstone and the Irish question as we drove to some isolated district for a service in a private home, discussed the life of Kipling as we tramped the shingle foreshore from Timaru to Pareora. He never patronised his children.

Dad was not a handyman despite his upbringing on the farm – he attempted to do everything with a single crescent spanner and a bulbous hammer – but he was something of an outdoors man: not club or team sports, nothing to do with machines, but in the mode of the literary walkers amongst the Lake Poets and the more serious New Zealand walkers like A. H. Reed, whom he much admired. He loved to walk, and walking was free; from his rambling boyhood in the kauri bush came a love of unspoiled country which never left him. He was happy to walk by himself, for that way he achieved privacy and time for thought and observation. At about 50 years of age he walked alone for several days through Molesworth Station and over the high watershed into the head of the Wairau River. In his clear but undramatic way, he described the dangerous force of the wind at the crest of the saddle and his need to push on. When I reflect on Dad's love of the outdoors, I'm surprised that

REVEREND ALAN JONES

he wasn't a devoted fisherman, because I know several people who use that pastime as a disguise for reflection and a love of nature. He was quite a good shot, for the family pot rather than sport, and shot a great many wood pigeons as a boy (when that was legal) and a great many rabbits later, but killing was for him always a necessity rather than a thrill. Neither was Dad much interested in organised sport, although he did follow cricket a little. I think he saw it as essentially frivolous. Although I enjoyed sport and played at minor provincial level in hockey and tennis, and others of the family had success, he never encouraged or congratulated us. Praise of any sort was rare from him: I think he saw in it the danger of fostering vanity.

He implanted in his family the qualities of self-reliance, intellectual curiosity, and an interest in the land around us. From an early age I often went camping with my brothers, biking with Barry the 60 kilometres from Blenheim to Pelorus Bridge, for example, when I was 11 or 12, and camping there for several days in a pup tent. There were tramping trips I took with Dad alone. When I was a university student, he and I walked around the top of the Coromandel Peninsula before the road was completed. I remember the lonely beaches with pohutukawa where we camped; and, one evening, an old shed which stood all alone and in which we slept less well than in the tent. We swam naked on beaches entirely deserted apart from ourselves. On the way back to Hamilton where the family then lived, I struck a fat, white farm duck with the Ford Consul, and Dad was torn between slight guilt and the considerable potential for the family pot.

During such open-air times, my father's talk was most likely to be that of a shrewd, natural philosopher. He would quote freely from his wide reading. He would talk of the need for a personal philosophy in life to give each individual the independence of his, or her, own mind.

I think, of all things, Dad abhorred a life of second-hand emotional responses and intellectual beliefs. Conventional, unexamined, received, mass views held no attraction for him. Everything was the better for being an individual outcome – a friendship, a book, the choice of a marriage partner, a sense of the natural world, a sense of God.

When we gathered as a family in 1989 to celebrate his eightieth birthday, he issued to us a typed sheet which held a summation of his personal convictions. The first tenet was 'I believe that life has meaning and purpose and is not merely an affair of blind chance', and his conclusion, 'These things I believe, however imperfectly I may have expressed them in words, or in life'. I joked with my brothers and sisters about it – such a typical formality of expression – but in private I reread it and envied the clear-eyed certainty with which he came to terms with life. My father had a sense of the isolation of human existence without giving way to despair on that account. This sense gave an essential gravity and calm to his attitudes and behaviour. He was in many ways a solitary man, but I don't believe he was a lonely one – his faith in things more important to him than people, or incident, saved him from that.

The aspect of my father most obviously influential on me was his love of literature. I came early to see that there was a life of the mind and to wish admittance so that I could share the fulfilment which he so clearly had discovered there. Both of us found it difficult to express emotion freely and our best means of making contact was a mutual appreciation of books. Largely self-educated, he had a reverence for scholarship and writing which is often the mark of those who have come late to learning, and despite obstacles. For him the great writers were the natural nobility of the world, and in our house the value of books was so unquestioned that it shook me to realise things could be different in other households.

Dad's study held many hundreds of books, almost all bought second-hand, which was perhaps one reason for his tastes being somewhat old-fashioned even then. As well as theology, the shelves held much fiction and poetry, and more history. He cared more for Gladstone and Disraeli than he cared for the politics of New Zealand in the 1950s. He loved the Lake Poets, Wordsworth in particular, and was one of the few men I have ever known, academics included, who would choose poetry for hours of recreational reading. He was steeped in the work of Hardy, Dickens, Scott, Galsworthy, Conrad and Stevenson. As my stepmother hurried about the house to get her work done, he would follow, mellifluously reciting from Lamb's essays, or quoting a quip from Boswell's life of Johnson. He was especially fond of Rudyard Kipling – the exotic British Raj attracted him, I think. He knew a great deal about Kipling's life and work, and sometimes was invited to give talks on the writer to community groups and institutions. I gather they were enjoyed. Apart from Fenimore Cooper, he never spoke much of other than British writers, and Somerset Maugham was the most recent author he seemed at all aware of in the 1960s. As would be expected in a self-educated literary man, his reading background was full of strange gaps and odd intensities. He knew many anecdotes drawn from the lives of nineteenth-century writers, and was familiar with the essays of Addison and Steele, yet he couldn't respond when I mentioned the work of Graham Greene or Robert Graves. I'm not qualified to comment on his grasp of theological books, but his love of John and Charles Wesley was clear. He knew that religion was of little interest to me, but would never force religion on anyone, despite the deep convictions he held. Whatever disappointment he felt about my lack of faith he kept to himself. Perhaps from the rock of his own Christianity he discerned my somewhat regretful agnosticism.

There was a lighter side to his reading. He enjoyed stories of colonial adventure; the Boer War seemed to figure strongly; and especially he loved Sherlock Holmes. He would read Conan Doyle to us as a family. Just a title, 'The Speckled Band' or 'The Dancing Men', will bring his voice back to me, bring back also the shape and feel of the kitchen in the Blenheim parsonage, and a host of less tangible associations. He had a tone of particular delight whenever the redoubtable brother Mycroft featured in a story.

My father's study seemed such a rich and settled place to me as a boy. The place of books, many of them annotated by my father or by previous owners. The Arthur Mee encyclopaedias, the history sets, the Everyman series, the leather-bound poetry and classics, the shoe boxes full of his sermon manuscripts, the heavy leather chairs, the dry fountain pens and kauri gum in his drawer, the hymn book and bible on the desk. They must have been very ordinary rooms from parsonage to parsonage, perhaps even threadbare, but even now as I enter them in imagination, I can sense the studious solitude and contentment which were pervasive there – an otherworldliness of fascinating dimension. On many occasions my father was happy to leave to my stepmother the bustle of a large family, ever-present housework, and uninvited guests, and enter his room of books. Particularly in later life, it was common for him to be found asleep there on a summer afternoon.

It's natural for a confirmed reader to want to write: Dad wrote both poetry and prose from a young man. I'm unsure of the amount or the intensity of his purpose, and wish I had talked to him more about it. I do recall, when I was a boy and he in his forties, that he wrote an adventure novel, 'The Treasure of Tuamotu', set in New Zealand and concerning Maori treasure, sailing ships, and moas. He sent it to publishers in Britain and New Zealand, and although some made favourable comment, none accepted it. I never gave a thought to the disappointment he must have felt, but of which he never spoke. He did have a few poems published in New Zealand periodicals such as *The Mirror*, among them 'My Neighbour's Wealth', which I include at the end of these recollections and which I remember him reciting to me long ago. Just a few years before he died, I wrote to him and asked him for a copy of it. He produced it from memory and his letter showed pleasure that I had asked for it. He put in some later poems as well. He would sometimes incorporate his poetry quite naturally within his preaching, and only if he was asked would he mention the authorship.

My own writing, or at least published evidence of it, did not occur until quite a few years after I had left home, and although I know he read the books and was tacitly supportive, we rarely had the opportunity or inclination to talk in depth of it. Occasionally I would hear indirectly of his enjoyment of something of mine. He and I maintained a sort of verbal semaphore, confining our talk to history, literature, and the natural world, in which we were sure of each other's opinions. He was stimulating in literary argument, and several times I noticed how shrewdly he had adapted his case from one joust to the next. A few times, when alone, we came on some difficult, deeply personal topic, and though his eyes would meet mine keenly, neither of us wanted to venture too far into vulnerable self-revelation. Dad valued his privacy and respected that of others. Even kinship was no excuse for prying. He approached my writing only obliquely in conversation: the scale of financial return seemed to interest him considerably, though I was able to reassure him that he had no reason for envy there. Once or twice he made comments about those stories which utilised our common experience, to show that the references hadn't escaped him. It interested him to see the process of distortion and selection by which life contributes to fiction.

I don't like to admit it to myself, but I think that in later years he lost something of his deep, literary passion, or perhaps he hesitated to express it amongst so many university-educated sons and daughters, even though none of us could match his facility in recalling quotation and source. There was also the disappointment, stoically endured as ever, of his own writing efforts, and a realisation that the books he loved had become old-fashioned. The colloquial, cynical style and amorality of many modern novels didn't attract him. Increasingly in old age his concern was with politics, particularly social policies which concerned the less well-off – himself included. He had a growing conviction that 'the rich' were in command, and on the infrequent occasions I saw him in his old age, the transgressions of oligarchies stirred him to his most vigorous expression.

My father was an excellent speaker and had a good baritone singing voice – I see him in my mind's eye cupping a hand to his ear to better hear himself singing and to deepen the tone. Often on a Saturday we would hear him practising the sermon for the next day, stopping and then repeating a sentence if he felt the cadence wasn't captured the first time. I imagine that he must have consciously trained his speaking voice to achieve a clear, neutral pronunciation. He had no tricks of speech, no pretensions, but his voice was considered and well-modulated, and he possessed a notable turn of phrase and a remarkable grasp of imagery and analogy. Within the New Zealand Methodist Church he was known as a powerful preacher, and many times people have told me the impact his sermons made upon them. His was neither a charismatic nor theatrical style, nor by any means dry; reasoned, logical, pictorial, enlivened with literary quotation and analogy from his own experience, and always impressive in its sincerity. As boy and man I never had occasion to feel anything but admiration for his speaking ability, and he was fortunate to maintain it well into his eighties.

Although not a garrulous man, Dad was a forthright and interesting talker when the time was right. He would draw on his wide reading, his Huckleberry Finn boyhood, the considerable experience of human nature that his work provided. His objective perceptiveness and quiet humour were in contrast with the egotism and second-hand gossip which dominated so much conversation. He was most at ease in the more formal situations: services, meetings, occasions of one sort or another, and least at ease in the social flux of a party or an outing. Certainly this was so in his later life. He had not much in the way of small talk, and often, I think, found little connection between his interests and those of the bulk of his compatriots. At such times I found him sitting quietly in the car, or off by himself in the garden. Boredom showed itself by his quiet withdrawal to the congenial company of his own thoughts, the countryside, or his books.

Like many men of his generation, Dad wasn't one to display feelings freely. I can't recall one kiss, hug, or overt statement of love for me, though his affection was clear in other ways. With his younger children, especially daughters Bronwyn, Rhonda, and Olwyn, with whom he had longer and closer contact, things were easier. It was a revelation to me to see the open warmth and unconditional emotional support which my wife, Jacqueline, gave to our own daughters, and I have tried hard to put aside my upbringing in this respect and become more like her. Perhaps partly as a consequence, Andrea and Belinda have been a joy to me.

No doubt it would have been undiplomatic for my father to talk much of my mother once he remarried, but there wasn't one instance when he thought to take me aside as boy or man, and tell me of the mother I never knew. A singular lack of empathy, it seems to me. The kindest interpretation I can place upon this is that such discussion would have woken too many painful memories for him. How typical of him, and how typical of our relationship, however, that almost without comment he once gave me a copy of *Great Expectations*, with 'Jane Jones, August 9th, 1939' inscribed on the flyleaf.

Even in those we know best, there are aspects of character and behaviour which baffle us. For most of the time he was in Blenheim, when he was in his forties, Dad raised and showed Old English Game fighting cocks, and won a national title with his prized The Earl of Derby. So ferocious were these roosters that they had to be kept in small pens of their own for much of the time. The hens were dowdy, but the males brilliantly coloured, elegant and strutting. I recall the fascinating but bloody process of 'dubbing,' in which the cocks had their combs and wattles removed. Dad used a razor blade for the purpose. The cocks were no longer fought of course, but enthusiasts such as my father raised them for conformity to ideals of the breed and delighted in their success at shows. Often the chicks were hatched in the warmth of the airing cupboard, and the best selected for exhibition. One particularly aggressive cock used to chase me and peck holes in my socks, until I learnt to land a kick. On one summer evening it fled down our street with Dad in hot pursuit, providing a good laugh for the neighbours at the usually composed Reverend Alan Jones. He would spend a good deal of time in the evenings standing before the individual hutches of his favourites, tucking up their wings and adjusting their posture with a wand. The hobby seems to me at variance with so much of his character. What did those gaudy birds represent, I wonder? What satisfaction had they for him at that stage of his life, for it was a fancy of a relatively few years. There were so many questions I never thought to ask while there was still the opportunity for answers.

In later years I thought more of him, in both senses, partly in awareness of his decline, partly in greater understanding of him as a mature man once I was middle-aged myself, partly because his failings are more pronounced in me, partly because a sense of family continuity increases in us in proportion to the realisation of our own transience. Life seems to me a twitchy business, but he twisted on the hook less than most of us.

My father's later life was saddened, or surely sobered somewhat, by the decline of religious faith and even superficial Christian observances in society. He and Barry, a former president of the New Zealand Methodist Conference, were only too aware of the comparison between the 1950s and the 1990s. Dad's churches in Blenheim and Timaru had been the centres of large congregations, thriving Sunday schools and Bible classes, youth camps, Boys' Brigades, study groups, dances, church picnics and concerts. And he held services in the small rural churches, most of which have now disappeared, or been converted to private homes. In his lifetime he saw religion becoming increasingly insignificant in society.

However, his own faith was strong, his nature optimistic, and his health excellent during a Wanganui retirement in which he continued to do much preaching and pastoral work until his eighties. He retained his mental powers until the end, and so was granted the last boon for which he prayed. I visited him twice in the year or so before he died, and although obviously much less physically active, he was still very much a whole man. On both occasions he told me that the only thing he feared was the loss of his faculties.

Death held no terrors for him whatsoever, and he died peacefully in his own home after a short illness and surrounded by his wife and all of his nine children except Rhys, who was serving overseas as a United Nations military observer and couldn't return in time. It was June 1995 and Dad was 85 years old. The day before he died, he and I talked briefly of climbing Mount Riley over 40 years before. He remembered it well. 'The mists closed in,' he said, referring to the fog which had prevented us from enjoying a view from the top.

Two or three years before Dad died, I woke from a dream of his death with tears still on my face. It occurred to me that the grief I felt may well have been a completely authentic response, and that dreams are one way in which we can have a certainty of experience about something which has never happened to us. The later grief was, as far as I could judge, identical. It is exactly the sort of question which would have interested my father, and for which he would have had a fund of apposite comment from his long ministry and his wide reading.

My Neighbour's Wealth

My neighbour's wealth is spread for me
In beauty of his almond tree.
I have no right by law of state
To share this glory by his gate;
And yet, unbought, it lifts for me
The branches gowned in witchery.

My neighbour owns, but I possess,
By virtue of receptiveness,
The beauty that is spread for me
Today upon his almond tree.

ALAN OSMOND JONES
(1909–1995)

While in Menton as Katherine Mansfield Memorial Fellow in 1996, and walking to the Villa Isola Bella in Garavan one hot day, the essential lines of the following poem came to me. I had not long before visited William Webb Ellis' grave in the hill cemetery of the old village.

Garavan

Today again I come to air the
small and unattended shrine
at Garavan.
And with me down that glaring
promenade – the Wesleyan from
Te Kuiti, Wekaweka and Timaru.

Quite, quite so he says, in
the temperate rationality of
his way.
Full of calm, introspective
strength, empty of violence, or
spite. He razor cut the combs

and wattles, dubbing, till the
keen, bloodied heads of his
Old English
Game came out. The scooters
shoot the tunnel under the old
town's rugby bones. Mysterious

cypress is revealed as just
a dapper macrocarpa after all.
Quite so.
There you lay, my Wesleyan
steady in your faith as ever
transfixed beneath that great

arrow of demise. Grief and memory
repressed, incandesce our myths
of fatherhood.
Isn't it enough to say, these days
no harm was done and none intended.

THE NUCLEUS HOLDING THE UNIVERSE TOGETHER

GREG NEWBOLD on *PETER NEWBOLD*

He's never talked a lot about his life, my dad. Not a man of many words; never a man for hyperbole. He doesn't get excited much either. I remember his reaction once when, at 13, I won the Auckland Judo Championship. When I told Dad he said, 'Good on you, Son. That's a feather in your cap'. And that was all. For Dad, that was high praise. Ten years later, I got arrested on a serious heroin charge in Auckland. I rang Dad from police headquarters and told him I was in jail. 'That's not too good, Son,' he said. For Dad, that signified deep disappointment. He's a taciturn sort of a bloke.

D ad was born in Eltham, Taranaki, in 1924. His father, Frank Newbold, was born in Wellington three years before the turn of the century. At 19, Frank went off to the First World War and when he got back, was balloted a farm in Taranaki by the government, under the Discharged Soldiers Settlement Act. Frank shared the farm with his older brother Norman, whom everyone called Trot because he never walked anywhere. But in the unstable economy of the 1920s times got tough for farmers and Trot started drinking, making things worse. One morning in 1922 it all blew up in the cowshed, and Trot and Frank started fighting. Trot lost the fight, but it was plain that the two could not keep working together. They tossed a coin for the farm; Frank lost, and he walked off. Without a penny to his name he asked Martha Jans, the girl over the road, to marry him. She accepted. They were wed in May 1922. Dad was born 18 months later.

Dad was raised in poverty. After he walked off the farm, Frank worked in a cheese factory, but when that went bust in the Depression he worked as a farm labourer and as a fencing contractor, earning what he could, when he could. For weeks at a time Frank was away in the bush of the King Country, cutting scrub and fence posts by hand and living off native pigeons and wild pork. Every few weeks he'd come home for a few days before disappearing into the hills again. Some of Dad's best childhood memories are of his school holidays, staying in the bush with his old man and shooting pigeons with an old .22 rifle.

But life at home was rough. Martha had seven kids and although the first died in infancy, keeping the other six on a labourer's wages was not easy. The kids' shoes were frequently worn through and padded up with paper. There was little money for schooling. As a teenager, Dad went to Wanganui Tech, but as soon as he was 15 he left and moved to Wellington, where he worked for a pound a week on an assembly line for a company called Radio Corp. From that time he was on his own, and everything he acquired later he earned himself. That had a significant impact on the way he brought us kids up. We had to work before we got paid, but Dad was determined that we would never experience poverty the way that he, and Mum, had.

Another aspect of Dad's life also affected the way he brought up his kids. Grandad was a tyrannical patriarch. The lord of the house when he was home, his wrath was feared by the whole family. At mealtimes, manners were so strictly enforced that the kids often trembled at the table. Discipline was swift and harsh. A sudden backhander corrected minor infractions; more serious offences earned a good hiding. As the eldest, Dad received more than his share. He learned fear at an early age. At five, he started school in an old single-room schoolhouse at Maungamahu, near Wanganui. The schoolmaster was a brutal man, and my father was terrified of him. Too frightened to go to school and too scared to tell his parents, one day Dad hid all morning in a culvert beside the road. Discovered by his mother, he was taken down to the schoolhouse where the schoolmaster gave him a prolonged thrashing with a leather strap. Dad was badly knocked around, and Frank beat up the schoolmaster for what he had done to his son.

This event traumatised my father, although he never talked much about it. But his violent upbringing had a huge influence on the way he brought us up. In the typical scenario, violence begets violence, and people who have been brutalised as children often become brutal parents themselves. Dad was the opposite. He swore to us that he would never thrash us the way he had been thrashed, and that he would never hit us with anything but his open hand. He kept his word, as he always did. A single whack on the bum was the only chastisement we ever got, although I can hardly ever remember it happening.

In Wellington after he had left school, Dad stayed with his three aunts, Lorna, Cath, and Hilda. His board was a pound a week, which was exactly what he earned, and he relied for any extras on money sent down by his mother. As a shy young man with an empty wallet, he didn't go out much and didn't have many girlfriends either. But working in the office at Radio Corp. was a young woman called June Elford. Slender, outgoing and beautiful, at 15 she already had many suitors. Dad worked with June's mother, Evelyn, on the radio assembly line, and one day at a work social, Evelyn introduced him to her daughter. Although his ribs showed through when he wore swimming togs, Dad looked pretty sharp in a suit, and June took a fancy to him. Precocious and confident, unlike Dad, June started to go out with him. But she continued to see other men as well, setting the tone for a long yet tense relationship.

They both had a few things in common. June was from Motueka, although her family was now living in Wellington. So in a sense she, too, was living away from home. Her father, Charles, was a carpenter and like Dad's, her family was poor. The Elford's house had burned down during the Depression and for some years they had lived in a big circus tent. June had known violence as well. Her mother had an uncontrollable temper and she used to beat June severely. At times June felt her mother wanted to kill her so, like my father, she knew the taste of fear.

In most other respects, Dad and June were opposites. June was extroverted; Dad was reserved. June loved the attentions of other men; Dad was only interested in one woman. June's sense of principle was relaxed and she seldom made moral judgements about others. Dad had a rigid moral code and he expected others to live up to it.

Nonetheless, the relationship grew and in 1949 they were married. June then shifted to Auckland, where Dad was then working. He had developed an interest in plan printing and in 1948 had been hired by a wealthy Auckland family to start a document reproduction business. The company became known as Neville Newcomb Ltd and Dad managed it for the rest of his working life.

I was the first child and came into the world in July 1951. At that time Mum and Dad were renting a tiny bach in the North Shore suburb of Takapuna, but soon after I was born we moved up the road to a cheap two-bedroomed flat. It is here, from about the age of two, that my earliest memories begin.

Dad didn't play a big part in my very early life. He worked long hours trying to get the business running, and until the Harbour Bridge opened in 1959, he had to catch a bus and a ferry to get to work on the other side of the harbour. Like most infants, I was attached to my mother. A new-age parent of the fifties, she believed in permissive parenting, in encouraging self-expression and creativity, and like Dad, she didn't believe in belting kids.

Mum and Dad had four kids in all – three sons and a daughter – and Dad left our upbringing to her. He trusted her judgement and they seldom argued about child-rearing matters. But they did squabble about money, which was tight, and about Mum's flirting. Whenever we had a party, Mum seemed to end up sitting on somebody else's knee. Dad would get agitated and after everyone went home, they'd fight about it. Mum had one or two affairs while she was married to Dad, but none of us kids really knew about them until later. Overall, they were both loving parents and our lives were pretty secure.

Dad liked to keep up appearances and he wanted people to know that his kids were well brought up and well cared for. Having good manners was big in his own upbringing and so it was in ours. But it was more important when we were in the company of others, and at an early age I learned that standards of behaviour and table etiquette were far more rigid when other people were watching than when we were at home by ourselves. Standards of presentation were equally important. Dad didn't want people to think that he couldn't support his family. Although we actually had hardly any money, we always had to have good clothes on when we went visiting and we could never have our photos taken without having our hair greased down and combed.

Coming from poor backgrounds made both Mum and Dad careful with money. By the time I was two, they had saved enough to buy themselves a second-hand four-cylinder Austin Seven. When Mum's parents and sister were killed in the Tangiwai train disaster in 1953, she inherited a little money as well and by 1956, when I was five, they had enough to put a deposit on a house. That year we moved to Northcote.

By the end of the 1950s, Neville Newcomb was prospering and Dad was on a reasonable wage, earning 20 pounds a week. The family had grown to six. My brother Rodney had been born in 1953, my sister Manda came in 1957, and two years later the last child, Vincent, arrived. We had a Volkswagen car and had enough money for an annual holiday. With some play-centre friends of Mum's, we used to camp on the cliffs above Goat Island Bay, near Leigh, and Dad would take Rod and me out fishing. Dad showed us how to rig a line and bait a hook, and how to get a struggling fish off a line. There were heaps of snapper around in those days and we always came back with plenty. In later years we camped on the deserted sandspit at the mouth of the Wade River. Dad wouldn't go near a camping ground because he hated crowds, and he instilled in us a love of the outdoors and open spaces. He also impressed on us the golden rule of camping: leave the place exactly as you found it.

Those holidays with Dad and Mum were magic. It was when we saw the most of Dad because a lot of the time he was working hard to build up the Newcombs' business and earn us money to live on. Often he worked on Saturdays, and during the week he was gone early in the morning and usually didn't get home until about 6 or 7 pm. We went to bed at 8 pm.

Sundays were always good. Dad would be home and on Sunday nights, to give Mum a break, he would cook tea. Dad was a great cook and we always looked forward to his meals. In the winter we'd often come home covered in mud from playing in the bush. Mum would run us a bath then we'd get into our pyjamas and have tea in front of the fire. Sometimes we'd play a trick on Dad and do something like put his dinner on his seat. He'd pretend he hadn't seen it and sit on his dinner then jump up with a yell of surprise. We'd laugh almost to tears.

After tea, especially on Sundays, Dad would sometimes play with us. Normally we'd have fights, and Rod and I would climb all over Dad and he'd growl and snarl and punch us on the shoulders. We'd drag him to the ground and bash him on the nose and he'd cover his head and pretend we'd beaten him. Before we went to bed he'd often give us a shoulder ride or be a horse and buck us off his back. We loved it. He'd do the same when we had visitors and play with their kids as well. The other kids used to say what a marvellous dad we had. I do the same with kids myself, now. I get on really well with children because of the lessons I learned from my old man.

Dad was the pillar of the family and he was our moral instructor. His

PETER
NEWBOLD

strength was so great and the respect we had for him was such that a harsh word was usually enough to make us do as we were told. He also impressed principles of honesty and reciprocity on us. If we borrowed money from him we always had to pay it back, and if we had a bet about something and lost, we always had to pay up. The handshake was a sacred and inviolable bond. Dignity, pride, and honour were qualities of paramount import-ance. Guilt was the major tool which Dad used to keep us honest. I could fool Mum into letting me take a sickie from school, but never could I fool Dad. He'd know if I was pulling one over Mum and he'd come in, look at me with contempt and say, 'You're not sick! What the hell's the matter with you?' Then he'd just walk out.

It made a sickie hardly worth taking.

Another thing that Dad impressed on us was the importance of admitting and apologising when we were wrong. He wasn't wrong that often, but when he was, he'd always come up afterwards and say, 'I'm sorry, Son. I made a mistake.' He also used to apologise if he'd lost his temper and made us go off crying. He never liked us to go to bed crying and he always came in to square things off before we went to sleep. Sometimes I'd get the sulks and refuse to talk to him. 'Oh, you're not going that way on me, are you, Son?' he'd say. 'I didn't think you'd go that way on your old man'. He'd try again and if I still refused he'd say, 'All right. Bugger you then'. And he'd walk out. That would always make me feel terrible and I'd wish he'd come back.

Dad was always consistent about discipline, but he wasn't inflexible. I remember once when I was about eight, my six-year-old brother Rod and I were playing in the outside washhouse and we began throwing water around. One thing led to another and pretty soon there was water everywhere, a few centimetres deep on the concrete floor. Dad came out and went crook at us and told us to clean it up. We started to, but then we began fooling around again and before long there was more water on the floor than before. Dad heard us laughing and skylarking and, seeing the cause, he got really irate and told us to clean up that bloody mess right now or else. So we started doing as he said, but once again we got distracted and started laughing and throwing water around. Then, to make my brother laugh more, I climbed up onto the bench and pissed into the water on the floor.

In walked Dad. Shit! I'd never seen him so mad. In a panic I ran for my life, out past him and up the big monkey-apple tree at the front of our section. Rod stood under the tree looking out for Dad, while I prayed that Dad wouldn't see me.

'Here he comes!' Rod called. Of course Dad knew where I was, it was the only big tree on the place, but he came out pretending to be looking for me. 'Where's that damned kid? Where is he, Rod? Where's Greg got to?' he demanded. 'I don't know, Dad,' Rod said. 'He's not up the tree'.

'No!' I thought. 'You've given me away!' I waited for Dad to order me down. But to my astonishment, he didn't even look up. I couldn't believe my luck! I sat there frozen and listened to Dad talking below. 'Well,' he said in his most menacing voice, 'you tell Greg that when I find him, I'm going to give him a bloody good hiding!'

Dad stalked off. As soon as the coast was clear I got down from that tree, and Rod and I raced around the back and cleaned that washhouse like it was new. Dad never said another word about it.

Until I was about 11 we had a fairly normal family life. Dad worked; we went to school; Mum looked after the house. But in 1962, things suddenly changed. The Ducat family came up from Tirau and moved into the rented house next door. They had three kids: Ranald, Kate, and the youngest, Andrew, who was my age and in my class at school. We immediately became good friends and so we are today. My mum also became friends with Andrew's mum, Gloria. That was the problem: Gloria and her husband, Sandy, were both alcoholics. Gloria was highly intelligent and well read, and Mum, who was intelligent but uneducated, looked up to her. Mum was also bored stiff with being a housewife. Dad had virtually prohibited her from getting a part-time job because he thought it would make him look bad. Moreover, due to Mum's precocity, Dad grew jealous and suspicious if Mum tried to develop any major interests of her own. But with Gloria now next door, Mum suddenly had someone stimulating to speak to on those dull afternoons before we got home from school. She'd go next door to Gloria's and talk about books or do the *Listener* crossword, or just gossip and laugh. Gloria would produce a flagon of cheap Old Pale Gold sherry and they'd have a few drinks. And a few more drinks.

From the time the Ducats moved next door, Mum began to spend more and more time with Gloria. Andrew and I would come home from school and it was common to find Mum and Gloria well on the way, laughing and smoking and drinking in Gloria's kitchen. We didn't care. We'd just grab a bite to eat then go off and have fun together. But by the time poor old Dad got home at 6.30 or 7.00 pm, Mum would be pissed as a chook. There would be no tea cooked and Andrew and I would be getting up to no good somewhere around the neighbourhood.

This was pretty devastating for my strait-laced, hard-working, traditionally minded dad. Mum would come home and abuse him for being a sanctimonious old bastard who could cook his own bloody tea and go to hell as far as she was concerned. In a matter of months, Dad's whole married life began to fall apart, and so did our life as a family. We stopped having holidays. We stopped doing things together. The fights between Mum and Dad were endless and sometimes finished in violence. Dad wasn't an aggressive man, but Mum was abusive and violent when she was drunk, and when she attacked Dad she usually ended up on the floor, crying and screaming that he was a bully. It happened time and time again. He only attacked her once when, in the desperate belief that it might change things, he gave her a methodical spanking. Mum was crying and pleading for him to stop, but it went on and on. Aged 12, I was absolutely mortified. He'd never done anything like that to us, but I knew how we could stop him. I got my brother and sister together and we took off into the night. We'd gone over a kilometre before Dad found us running down a side street. He pleaded for us to get into the car. He said he was sorry and it would never happen again. It never did, but Mum's bum was black and she didn't change at all.

Dad continued to try and salvage the marriage. When I was 13, we moved out to Mairangi Bay, where Dad hoped the link with alcohol would be broken. He was concerned about me, too. I was commencing my growth spurt into young adulthood and starting to define my own needs and wants. They were different from Dad's. I wanted to grow my hair long; Dad wanted me to get it cut. He didn't want people to think his son was a lout and he tried to get me to dress and behave the way he thought was appropriate. But I hated his taste in clothes and I liked long hair. Arguments became common and tensions between us grew.

One day it all blew up. It happened on the day of the opening of Mangere Airport in January 1966. I was 14. A huge air pageant had been organised to mark the transfer of Auckland's airport from Whenuapai to Mangere. Dad loved aeroplanes and he asked me if I wanted to go with him. By now I was hardly ever spending time with Dad, so I was really looking forward to it. The morning of the pageant dawned fine and sunny, but it was obviously going to be a real stinker; one of those hot and humid days when your clothes stick to your skin and your feet cook. I dressed in a light shirt, clean denim beach shorts, and jandals. Dad appeared dressed in long pants and shoes, and when he saw me he was not pleased. 'You're not going like that,' he announced. 'You can put on some decent clothes like me. My friends are going to be there and I'm not taking you anywhere looking like a bloody hooligan.'

I was flabbergasted and outraged. He wanted me to wear long pants and shoes and by-the-way-it-was-about-time-I-had-another-haircut! He wanted a son he could be proud of in front of his mates; I wanted to be myself, and I didn't want to be hot and clammy all day. I tried to reason with him, but he was absolutely intransigent. Before long we were yelling at each other. He said I had to do as I was told. Close to tears, I shouted that I wasn't going to go at all. He ordered me to get changed and come with him. I snapped, exploding with tears and frustration, and ran downstairs to my room in a state close to hysteria. I'd made my mind up I wasn't going now, no matter what, and he was enraged at my defiance. Upstairs, he and Mum started arguing about who was right, and then I heard him say, 'He's coming with me, and that's final!' And he started down the stairs.

Our old .22 rifle was sitting in my wardrobe. I grabbed the gun and I loaded it. Dad burst into the room: 'Get in that damned car!' he yelled.

I could hardly see for the tears. 'Fuck off!' I screamed, levelling the gun at his chest. 'Get out of here you fucking bastard or I'll fucking kill you!' I was out of control – I really meant it.

Dad saw the madness in my eyes and backed out of the room. For what seemed an age, I sat on my bed with the loaded gun in my lap, sobbing and shaking with rage. Mum came in. I picked up the gun. 'Put down the gun, Son,' she said. 'Your father says he's sorry. He really wants you to go with him. You can wear what you want'. I burst into tears again, while Mum talked softly to me. When I'd calmed down a bit, Dad came down and stood humbly in front of me. 'I'm sorry, Son,' he said. 'I was wrong to try and tell you what to wear. There's nothing wrong with what you've got on. Those shorts are quite nice, really. Come on, old mate, come with me to the air pageant. We'll have a great day.'

I'd never seen my Dad look so hurt and remorseful in my life before. I agreed to go with him to the pageant, and we had a marvellous day.

But as far as Mum's drinking was concerned, the move to Mairangi Bay didn't make much difference. Mum couldn't pop next door so easily but sometimes after school and on most weekends she would drive the 12 kilometres to Gloria's. I'd go too, because I wanted to see Andrew, who was my best mate. While Andrew and I smashed power cups with our shanghais or went down the bush hunting opossums, Mum would pop valium and drink sherry with Gloria, then drive us home. Some days were worse than others, but on bad days she'd be blind drunk. With the car full of kids, she would career wildly onto the opposite side of the road, up the footpath, into road signs. Amazingly, we never had a serious accident, although we got hauled out of one or two ditches and Mum hit the side of the house a few times trying to come down the driveway. She lost her licence twice.

At home, our lives were now pretty well dominated by Mum's drinking. As a young teenager I was mostly doing my own thing by this stage, and her alcoholism was not a major concern. But every night when Dad came home, the fights would start. Night after night after night. Mum and Dad fighting. Sometimes verbal, sometimes physical, depending on how drunk she was. The tension appeared as soon as Dad walked in the door, and we kids just waited for the sparks to start flying.

Knowing his marriage was over, Dad began to withdraw from the relationship. For about a year we hardly saw him. He'd leave early in the morning and come home after we'd gone to bed. He always came home, but it was always late. He didn't eat at home and did his laundry at the YMCA. Finally, one night late in 1967, after yet another argument, he just packed a few things and walked out the door. He was almost in tears as he said goodbye to his family and to his marriage of almost 19 years.

I was 16. I didn't feel much at all. We'd hardly seen Dad for months and we knew the breakup was coming anyway. I just felt a great relief that the arguments were finally over and I looked forward to growing my hair.

So, from my point of view at the time, Dad's departure wasn't a bad thing. Since Mum had no control over me, I was now able to do more or less whatever I wanted at a time when most youngsters want to do just that. I studied hard at school but on weekends I'd go out with my cobbers, boozing and partying and being the lout that my father never wanted me to be. Our house at 110 Sunrise Avenue became a regular party venue, with scores of teenagers arriving on motorbikes and in clapped-out cars carrying dozens of beer and bottles of Screwdriver. Mum would be down the pub or somewhere with one of her boyfriends – by the time she got home the party would be in full swing. As long as we gave her a dozen beer she'd be cool. Then we could all get drunk, have a good time and wreck the house.

Dad's departure from the family home not only altered my personal life, it also marked a dramatic change in our relationship. He moved into a flat in Takapuna, then to one in Belmont, and every Wednesday we'd go around there for tea. Dad would cook something delicious or we'd have Chinese takeaways, which were a real treat back then. We saw more of Dad now than we had before, and it was quality time. Best of all, he stopped trying to organise my identity and just seemed to like me the way I was. It was as if he stopped trying to be a father and started being my mate. I felt I could talk to him about anything and I knew he would stick by me without passing judgement.

A few months after he left, his new role was put to the test. Still aged 16, I was having my first love affair, with a girl down the road called Cherry who was two years older than me and worked in a local bank. Early one morning her old man, a big Welsh bulldozer driver, caught me sneaking out of her bedroom window. He charged at me from behind, roaring with rage and punching me in the head with his fists. I managed to break free and took to my scrapers, but three nights later I got another hiding, this time from an older guy who was competing for Cherry's affections. Then two days after that, I got kicked out of school. Cherry's parents were Open Brethren and so was the chairman of the Board of Trustees of Rangitoto College, where I was in the sixth form. Through him, Cherry's parents got the headmaster, Frank Tucker, to boot me out for the 'grossly immoral conduct' of knocking off their daughter.

It wasn't a good week. My face was bruised from two beatings and

GREG AND PETER NEWBOLD, 1970

now these idiots were trying to destroy my education. I was doing well at school, studying hard for my UE. I wanted to go to university, so I had to stay at school. But Tucker had me blacked from all the other schools in the district. I was in deep shit. Mum stuck by me and she took me down to see Dad. He knew I was being screwed and said he'd support me in any way he could. But my only chance of getting back to school was to square off with the board and with the headmaster.

In the end a deal was worked out whereby I had to write a letter to the board apologising for my wicked conduct and for the damage I'd done to the reputation of the school. I also had to promise never to see Cherry again. Then, dressed in a jacket and tie borrowed from Dad, I had to go with Mum up to the school one night, apologise to Frank Tucker in person and humbly ask to be allowed back to school. After letting me sweat for a few more days, they did allow me back and I got my UE, but I hated Tucker's guts from that point on.

After Dad left, we all sort of went our own ways. The Supreme Court awarded Dad custody of Vince, who was only 10, and he went to live with Dad. My sister Mandy struggled on at home but eventually left school after getting her School Certificate. Rod got his UE, and one of Mum's boyfriends jacked him up a job labouring in a timber yard. I grew more and more rebellious and kept kicking back at authority. The day I got my UE accredited, I was charged for shooting holes in some 'No Shooting' signs at Piha beach.

In 1969, early in the seventh form, some mates and I got drunk at the school ball and pissed all over the school's velvet emblem in the assembly hall. Soon after this, three of us were told by Tucker to have our hair cut short or leave. We left. Through his brother who worked for the Forest Service, Dad fixed me up with a job as a hunter-workman in the Ruahine Ranges. Once there, I shaved my head bald and sent a photo to Tucker.

When I left the Forest Service at the end of winter, I joined the Fire Service as a firefighter and was stationed at Parnell. I didn't get on too well in a regimented occupation. I got in trouble for calling the deputy chief fire officer 'mate' instead of 'Mr Bruce', for having women in my room at night, for suspected drinking on duty and for pouring hair oil over the lino in the corridor to the engine room so everyone fell over when the bells went. Finally, I had a fight with a senior fireman over who was going to ride in the number one position on the pump. Because I was known as a rebel I got the blame, even though he'd hit me first, and they transferred me to the Central Auckland firestation to keep an eye on me. At Central the authority was even worse, so I decided to leave and go to university.

By this stage I was smoking marijuana and had taken my first LSD trip. Dad could see me changing but as an absentee parent – and in any case, because of the way I was – there was little he could do about it. It must have been hard for him, being as conservative as he was, but he'd given up trying to moralise to me. When I went to court for shooting up the signs, he'd tried to impress on me the significance of what was happening. 'Don't you realise what you've done?' he said. 'You've broken the law of the land, Son!'

'So what?' I replied. 'I don't give a shit about the law of the land.'

There wasn't much he could say. He couldn't comprehend my lack of shame or remorse. He couldn't understand why I liked wearing torn old jeans instead of 'nice' clothes. Once, he bought me a nice shirt and nice walk shorts for Christmas. I never wore them. When I turned 21, he shouted me to a flash restaurant and lent me a suit to wear. 'Now you look real smart,' he said. 'Doesn't that feel good?' As a student living off 20 dollars a week, I enjoyed this taste of luxury, but really it wasn't me. A week later, at my own twenty-first party, I got blind drunk, borrowed

Mum's car without telling her, rolled it and wrote it off: that was more my style. I thought that pranging a car was the best thing that could have happened on my birthday, and because it was insured it didn't even cost me a cent. What a bonus!

I worked my way through university and didn't have to take money from my parents. Dad had always taught us the importance of self-reliance. But still, I knew I could always count on him for a loan if things got tough. In the summer of 1970–71, I went to Australia with some mates. Dad took me out to the airport and picked me up when I came back. I'd had a great time and earned enough dough to see me through the year. I also brought back some marijuana seeds hidden in my camera, and planted them in a baked bean can to see what would happen. They grew. I told the next-door neighbour. She called the cops. I got busted.

The cops burst in the door one night in March 1971 and just about gave poor old Mum a heart attack. She staggered back, shaking with fright as the coppers barged through the house looking for the big marijuana plantation they'd heard about. They soon found the plants in the baked bean tin and a tiny bit of hooch in a sandshoe. With grave looks they arrested me and Rod, who was 16 at the time. Denied police bail, we spent the night in the cells at Central Police Station. Dad picked us up at court the next day. Rod was charged with simple possession and got fined, but I faced a cultivation charge which carried a 14-year maximum sentence.

Cultivating cannabis was considered pretty serious in those days and there was always a chance that I would lose my liberty. I thought the law's view of the matter was bullshit and told this to Dad, who said nothing, and to my probation officer, who wrote it all down. Unfortunately, this probation officer was the father of a schoolmate of mine and knew a bit about my history. He wrote in his report that I was headstrong, uncontrolled, unrepentant, and in need of corrective discipline. He recommended three months in a detention centre. Jim McLay, who later on succeeded Rob Muldoon as leader of the National Party, represented me, arguing that to lock me up would ruin my year at university. But the magistrate, an old war vet, felt that discipline was more important than study, so off I went to jail.

Arrival at the Waikeria detention centre was a rude introduction to prison life. Waikeria was modelled on the military boot camp. We started off by having our heads shaved almost bald. Our daily routine consisted of quick-marching all over the place in formation, working knee-deep in mud, and being kicked, clouted, sworn at and put on report for trivial offences like having a cell that wasn't spotless, marching out of step, or farting in the mess room. I'd never seen anything like it and at first I couldn't believe it. Mum and Dad came down together to see me on the first weekend and told me that Jim McLay had put in an appeal against sentence. It was eventually heard by Justice Speight in the Supreme Court, and the sentence was replaced by four months' residential periodic detention.

It didn't take long to get over the shock of jail and back into the swing of things. One Sunday after PD, my mate Andrew and I pinched some of Mum's valium. We swallowed 100 mg each, just for fun, and went for a ride on Andrew's Vespa 150 scooter. In Mairangi Bay we crashed into a rubbish bin on the footpath, fell over and couldn't get up. Somehow we got home and remained virtually comatose for the next 24 hours. When I came to, Mum rang Dad to get him to talk some sense into me. I was still only half conscious and yelled at him that he didn't know what he was talking about and to mind his own bloody business. I remember him saying, 'Greg! Greg! This is your father! This is your father you're speaking to!' 'I don't give a fuck who you are!' I shouted. 'I'll do whatever I fucking well feel like and you don't tell me what to do! So you can just fuck off!' Then I hung up and went to sleep for another 12 hours.

A couple of days later, after I'd come around properly, Mum told me what I'd said and I vaguely recalled the conversation. When Mum told me how much I'd hurt my father, I was deeply, deeply ashamed. He'd always done the best he could for me. How could I have treated him like that? I rang him up and apologised in the most sincere way I could, but I really didn't know what to say. I tried to explain that I had been out of my head. But I'd said what I'd said, and for months I was plagued by a terrible guilt.

In 1970, Dad had married a beautiful woman called Diane, who had worked for him for years at Neville Newcomb. Diane is 20 years younger than Dad, but they are perfectly suited. She was brought up a strict Catholic and is even more conservative than Dad. Like him, she is scrupulously honest, with a powerful sense of dignity and fairness. They have almost never argued in over 25 years of marriage, and Dad adores her.

Diane coming onto the scene changed our relationship with Dad, because he had someone else in his life and soon started a second family. Only Vince, the youngest of us kids, was invited to the wedding; I think because of the fact that Diane isn't much older than the rest of us. Personally I would have liked to be there, but I accepted that it was their day, not mine. Dad also returned to Catholicism, which surprised me even more. Although he had been raised as a Catholic, he had always been an atheist with us. I felt he made the conversion to please Diane and make himself acceptable to her family.

Initially, I think, Diane had difficulty relating to us, especially me, because I was so different from her. But Dad had one uncompromising rule: he had a sacred duty to all of his kids. Diane accepted that and she accepted what Dad had always said to us – that his home was our home and we were welcome in it whenever we wanted. I never questioned his sincerity about this and never had cause to. Diane, for her part, did her best to accommodate us and gradually she and I became good friends. A woman of great strength, impeccable honesty, and rigid integrity, she has precisely the same qualities that I admire in my father.

But back in the early 1970s, I was still in my wild years and getting wilder. I left home in 1971 because I couldn't study with Mum's drinking, and went flatting in Parnell, then Grafton, which was the centre of Auckland's hippie culture. Like many other students, I got deeper into the drug scene and in 1973 I started dealing in marijuana. Then I began injecting hard drugs and selling them as well. After years of frugality, I suddenly had heaps of money and, instead of arriving on my old Vespa, I roared up to Dad's place for lunch on the odd Sunday on a late model Triumph Bonneville 650. Wearing velvet bell-bottoms and a paisley waistcoat, I would have a silk scarf around my neck and a big gold hoop in my ear. I was dead cool. Dad didn't think so. When Dad saw the big earring he just said, 'What the hell's that? Oh, Gawd!'

If Dad suspected what I was doing, he didn't mention it. There was absolutely no point. I knew it all in those days and nobody could tell me anything. Dad was just hoping I would grow out of it before I did myself any damage. But that wasn't to be.

In July 1975, a week after I turned 24, I got busted for selling an ounce of heroin to an undercover cop. I was interrogated for a few hours and said nothing, and for the next four-and-a-half months was held on remand at Mount Eden Prison. In November, I was sentenced to seven-and-a-half years' imprisonment and transferred to the maximum security prison at Paremoremo.

Dad was shattered – his worst nightmare had come true. The case got wide press coverage and my name was in all the papers. But now, more than ever, he felt the need to stand by me. My eyes welled with tears when I saw him walk through the grille on the first visit to Mount Eden, and he wept too, on the other side of the glass barrier which separated us. He organised me a lawyer, Peter Williams, and visited me religiously throughout my remand period. Mum did as well. By this time she was living with a Welsh guy called Eddie, who had been locked up in a boys' reformatory in Wales for four years when he was a kid. He treated me like family, and on the days when Dad didn't come up, Mum and Eddie would visit me.

In prison, with the rest of my twenties pretty well shot, I had to make some serious choices about what I was going to do with my life. I knew that my best chances lay in completing my degree, so that my time would not be entirely wasted, and hoping I could make a go of it when I got out. And that is what I resolved to do.

Studying inside prison isn't easy, however, and it requires a lot of running around on the part of others in order to get reading and research material. In this regard the library at Auckland University was tireless in its efforts, and Dad and Mum both pitched in wherever necessary. While I was in maximum security, and close to Auckland, Dad and Mum would alternate to make sure I got a visit every week, without fail. Dad also organised my mates to visit me on some weekends, and my brother Rod, who by then was living in Tauranga, would come up whenever he was in town. In jail I took up woodcarving and leather work, and it was Dad who ran around Auckland buying me the tools I needed, getting totara logs, hides, and books of patterns and designs. At Christmas time, when inmates were allowed a Christmas parcel containing specified items like aftershave, cake, confectionery, and biscuits, Dad would arrange mine. And once they wised up to the visiting routine, Mum or Dad would sometimes bring a little flask of whisky for me to slug down while nobody was looking. Poor old Mum would get so jumpy before she did it that she had to have a few good hits herself, to calm her nerves. One day which became infamous in the prison, Mum had a few hits too many and crashed over on her back in the visiting room, sending the bottle of grog spinning across the floor.

She was marched down to the superintendent's office by a couple of screws, abusing them all the way for being a pack of bastards and locking up her beloved son. Jack Hobson, the superintendent, a good old bloke with a sense of humour, just banned her from the prison for a month.

Halfway through my sentence, much to Dad and Mum's pride, I finished my MA thesis on the social organisation of prisons, won first-class honours, and got transferred from Paremoremo to the minimum security camp at Hautu, near the southern shores of Lake Taupo. Mum and Eddie were in England by this time, on a working holiday, but Dad or Rod would visit me once a month. They were allowed to bring a picnic lunch for us to eat in the gardens, and of course they always brought a bottle of grog as well, hidden in their clothing. I'd call one of my mates out and we'd all have a feed and a few drinks and mellow out for a while. When Mum and Eddie came back, near the end of my lag, they did the same. The screws didn't seem to mind too much, as long as you didn't get mouthy or stagger about when you walked back into the compound at the end of the day.

During my last stretch at Hautu, I became eligible for 72-hour home leaves every two months. The idea of home leaves is to reintegrate you into your family prior to release. Fairly tight conditions are laid down: you must not consume alcohol or any other drug, must not associate with criminals (and by now most of my mates were criminals), and must stay with your sponsor the whole weekend. Dad agreed immediately to be my sponsor, but I knew that Diane would not have been at all happy about me bringing women around for the night, especially the kinds of women I knew. In other words, the parole conditions meant no drink, no drugs, no mates, and no sex. 'Well, fuck that,' I thought, and I came to Auckland on my first leave without the slightest intention of respecting my parole conditions. On all my home leaves from then on, I would spend some time with Dad, but in the evenings I'd hit the pubs and clubs and parties of Auckland, drinking and playing up with my old jail mates, and entertaining the various females who came my way. I never came home at night and it was great. Poor old Dad didn't know what to do: he just sighed, and said, 'Be careful, Son,' and made me promise to ring him at least once a day so he'd know I was okay. I could understand why he was worried and I knew the risks I was taking, but not having had sex for five years made me about as cautious as a red stag in the rut. What could I do?

Fortunately I never got sprung breaching parole and in July 1980, I came to Auckland on work parole. I was finally discharged on 30 October, nearly five-and-a-half years after being busted. I knew Dad was worried, with good reason. I started flatting in Ponsonby with some people I knew from jail and I was a real loose cannon, drinking and womanising every night as if I was trying to make up for five years of deprivation in a month. On my first day out I shot up some heroin in a pub toilet, and a few days later, scored some LSD and methamphetamine at a bikie party. I bought a car and wrote it off within a week. I got into a bloody fight with a bouncer in a nightclub and ended up at Auckland Hospital, then Auckland Central Police Station. Fortunately, because the bouncer had pulled a knife on me first, I wasn't charged. Then the prostitute I was going out with got pregnant, and a junkie woman I was seeing on the side got pregnant as well. Fortunately, both had abortions. Life was pretty fast in those first few weeks. But it was clear, even to me, that I was living a charmed existence and that my good luck could not last. I didn't want to go back to jail. I detested jail and I didn't want to put poor Mum and Dad through all that shit again. I had to slow down.

Luckily, I had some pretty strong and dedicated supporters, apart from Mum and Dad. Bernie Brown, an associate professor of law at Auckland University, had got me a temporary job at the university and had vigorously supported my application for a postgraduate scholarship so I could do a PhD. Bill Hodge, then a senior lecturer in law at Auckland, began taking me out for long-distance runs and prepared me for my first marathon, late in 1980. I also began to box, and won a couple of amateur bouts in the first half of 1981. So, by early that year, I had begun to train quite seriously, had a job, and had taken up a scholarship to start studying in earnest for my doctorate.

Now that I had direction in my life, Dad breathed a sigh of relief. When my PhD was submitted five years later, I could tell how proud Dad was of me. 'Good on you, Son,' he said, and he shook my hand.

In 1987, I landed a job as a lecturer in sociology at Canterbury University. Now I'm a senior lecturer and I have a daughter of my own. Mum died of cancer in 1995, but before she died, she married Eddie and stopped drinking. During the few months of life she had left, I got to know once again the mother who had been the focus of my existence during my early years of life. It was a precious time for me, and it made me realise how hard it's going to be when Dad goes as well.

These days I ring Dad regularly, and I see him several times a year, when I'm in Auckland doing research or passing through on my way to overseas conferences. I'm more conscious now than ever before of what fathers mean to the way a person turns out, because everything that I am today has in some way, subtly or otherwise, been influenced by my father's steady, unwavering input. So it is for all of Dad's kids. He taught us to love one another and to stick together when times get tough. All of my family stood by me when I was in jail, and since my release, we've been closer than ever. We almost never argue or bitch at each other. Our homes are open and we love seeing each other when we can. Dad and Diane, their two kids Sarah and Paula, Mum's husband Eddie, Mandy and her husband Rick, Vince and his wife Jean, Rod, and all our kids, are part of this circle of people to whom we are committed, because we are family and because we love our family.

It was Dad who instilled within us this important principle of togetherness. Dad and Mum created our universe. Dad was the nucleus who held the universe together. Today, with his kids grown up and getting older, Dad and Diane remain at the centre of our world. When Dad dies, Diane will still be there. She will orchestrate the family and help preserve the principles of honour and integrity which have featured throughout our father's life. These principles will be preserved by us and hopefully, if we follow Dad's example, they will be transferred to our children.

Après le déluge, moi
Letter to my Father
from his Youngest Son

Nicholas Reid on *John Reid*

Dear Dad,

I was at a film festival screening at the Civic last year, coming down one of the broad staircases, when I met Professor Pooter coming up. He greeted me in a friendly fashion and we got talking. I was flattered. He still remembered me, even though it must have been 25 years since I sat, as an undergraduate, in his tutorials. But when a third person came along he introduced me thus: 'This is . . . um, er, um, ah . . . John Reid's son.' In fact, he hardly remembered me at all. He remembered me only in connection with you.

I won't pretend this sort of thing happens all the time. You died in 1972, your memory isn't green, and I suppose I don't mix all that often with your contemporaries. But when it does happen, it stirs up the strangest mixture of pride and annoyance in me. I'm proud to be your son. I'm proud of who you were, what you were, the battles you fought and the things you stood for. At the same time, I'm annoyed by the 'son of . . .' tag. It seems like a reproach, as if I haven't made enough of a mark on the world to be given a name. And then I'm annoyed at myself for being annoyed at something so trivial. After all, I really am 'son of . . .' I am reminded of it every day. When Mum moved out of the family home some years back, I probably looted more of your library than any of my siblings. About a third of the books on my extensive shelves once belonged to you, so your literary taste greets me from the walls whenever I get up, and whenever I sit at my desk to write something. I easily drift back in memory to the time (I must have been 12 or 13 years old) when I took great pride in knowing where every volume was on your shelves, and pointing it out to you when you had lost something.

Over the last two or three years, I have become aware of a number of superficial demographic ways in which we are alike. Like you, I still go to Mass every Sunday, and that is even more of a minority activity now than it was when you were alive. You had seven children (me being the youngest). My wife Gabrielle and I have seven children. And yes, dammit, I do teach English and I probably read far too many books.

None of these things was inevitable and none was planned in conscious emulation of you. Nor am I laying claim to a unique likeness to you. I am only one seventh part of your inheritance, and each of your six sons and one daughter reflects some aspect of you (and Mum) in quite different ways. None of my six siblings has a domestic situation exactly like mine and, if put to the task, each of them would write about you in quite different ways from the way I am writing here. But, unbidden and unplanned, the likenesses are still there, and I now wonder if it has to do with the fact that I was only 20 when you died. Did my siblings (all older than me) get a chance to lock horns with you, chop logic with you, disagree with you, agree with you, stand up to you, speak to you as adult to adult, in ways that I never did? I was only on the verge of real adulthood when you went. I can remember having a few sullen teenage spats with you, but nothing serious; nothing on the level of the bellowing barneys I know you had with at least some of my older brothers.

Perhaps they were getting the measure of you, and working out exactly who they were in relation to you. Perhaps I assimilated some of your ways, never really got to challenge or question them to your face as a grown-up, and proceeded to imitate them. Perhaps I've lost a vital stage in psychological development. The only time I had any real success in creative writing, I produced a series of short stories for radio about my early childhood which, in retrospect, seem Edenic and idealised, as if I didn't want to face the less pleasant bits of adolescence and adulthood. I could add another row of 'perhapses' at this point as well. But here I am, your son, Catholic, philoprogenitive, bookish, and a bit baffled by the experience.

When I think of you now, it's still with a sense of loss. In a general way, I'm sorry that you never met my wife and were never a grandfather to our children. Sometimes I'll be reading a book – most often a nineteenth-century classic – and be sorry I can't discuss it with you. Recently, I was trudging through Thackeray's *The Newcomes*, and I came to the part where quixotic Colonel Newcome shows he would proffer any excuse, meet any hardship or make any sacrifice on behalf of his mediocre, dozy son, Clive. The lit. crit. side of me (part of your inheritance) instantly recognised this as Victorian twaddle; but I still felt like bawling about it – an image of father-son love that carries on into adulthood.

You were only 56 when you died, in mid-career and mid-controversy. You were two years short of your hero, Dickens. Your eldest son is now older than you ever were; junior academics from your time have grown old or retired; and I have to put you together from childhood and teenage memories that are probably no more reliable than anyone else's.

Where to begin?

The smell of pipe smoke from the pipe always clenched in your mouth; the panama hat in summer; the chin scratched thoughtfully or sceptically while you puckered your lips over the book you were reading or the article you were annotating; everybody who remembers you remembers these things, and they were a reality. More strongly, though, I remember your sense of urgency and rush. You were always in the middle of doing something and always running to keep appointments. Your dismissive cry of 'Bunkum!' (or, *in extremis*, 'Balls!') was the cry of a man who did not have the time to waste on nonsense. Every one of your children could impersonate you running for the front door, patting your pockets and frantically muttering 'Where are my keys? Where's my pipe? Where's my wallet?'

From earlier childhood I can remember your expanding belly, warm and ready for me to fall asleep against as I was squeezed between Mum and you in the front seat of the Ford Prefect on long car journeys, with the older kids squeezed into the back. I remember you wading in your cross-hatched black-and-gold bathing trunks, big-bellied, pipe still clamped in your mouth as your feet played with the waves. And that belly again – it heaved up and down in hilarity as you lounged back in a chair watching some crude British sitcom. I once put a book on your laughing belly to see it bounce. This made it heave even more. Then there were those bearish outbursts of good fun – the late twilight when you played roly-poly, like a big kid, with Godfrey (17 months my senior) and me in the long grasses of the horse paddock at the bottom of the street, before they pushed the highway through. The pride we felt when, as small children, we accompanied you to film previews – 'You'll be the first children in New Zealand to see this' – although it's odd for me to reflect that I've now been writing film reviews for approximately five times longer than you ever did.

Then there was your encouraging, conspiratorial wink that told me the world and its shibboleths were really a joke, and the judgements of some adults did not have to be taken seriously. I can date quite specifically my first memory of this wink. I was nine. You had been roped in to play Santa Claus at some Christmas party for the offspring of university staff. At some point in the proceedings you disappeared, to re-emerge in costume with a cotton-wool beard and Mum's lipstick dabbed on your cheeks for Santa's rosy complexion. When you gave out the presents from your sack, I happened to be the last kid to get one. You rumpled my hair, gave me both the present and that conspiratorial wink, and said, 'Here, this is for you, you horrible kid,' as you departed. Your tone of voice conveyed 'you horrible kid' as a term of the deepest affection. I got a double laugh when you came back as yourself a few minutes later: one of your colleagues' younger sons (a couple of years younger than me) enthusiastically told you that he had just met Santa Claus. This made me feel awfully superior. Even at that age I had too many wicked, tattle-tale older brothers to harbour any illusions about Santa Claus. Even funnier, though, a childless woman present protested to Mum that you absolutely and definitely should not have addressed one of the children as 'you horrible kid'. Your wink told me how wrong she was and how silly other adults could be, and I never forgot the lesson. The wink would come back when you shared the corniness of a joke or deflated the pretensions of academic chatter.

Without entirely meaning to, you gave us some interesting lessons in civics, too. You were made properly uncomfortable by the way some people deferred to you, like the picture-theatre manager who bustled over and said, 'You don't have to pay, Doctor Reid', when you were trying to treat us to the movies in the holidays. Or the young traffic cop who basically broke the law for you – he must have been wet behind the ears. We had been for one of those joint family picnics on the black sand of a west coast beach – Piha or Muriwai, I forget which, as I was only 10 or 11 at the time. You had spent the long afternoon talking to your friends and drinking wine, and on the journey back across Auckland you were, shall we say, merry. The car weaved a little. The young cop stopped you and asked to see your licence. You gave it to him and he scrutinised it very carefully. Eventually he asked, 'Do you really teach at the university?' You nodded, whereupon he snapped a very smart salute and took off. We continued merrily home.

I can't help feeling now that the fellow misread your status and didn't imagine how embarrassed his leniency would make you. A decade later, you were for the second (and, as far as I know, only other) time over the legal limit in charge of a car and had your licence suspended. That time your embarrassment really was palpable. I had been out to see a movie with some student mates. You and Mum were supposed to have gone to an opera, so I was surprised to find you at home before me. Sheepishly, you told me that you had never made it to the opera. In the early evening you had indulged more than you realised at some wine-tasting, and had been stopped on the motorway. This was only a couple of months before the last heart attack, so you never drove a car again.

I can't say that I ever knew you to be drunk, and I think you would have regarded habitual drunkenness as ridiculous. But two or three times I do remember seeing you, through my reproving teenage eyes, being very silly over the wine at dinner parties. 'Block your ears, Nicholas,' you said on one such occasion, 'I'm going to tell a rude joke.' You needn't have worried – I'd heard that particular joke at school about three years earlier.

I have a chaos of miscellaneous impressions of your tics and peculiarities – things that teach no lesson but are memorable to me.

Your Francophilia. The volumes of Bernanos and Mauriac and Bloy and Peguy testified to that, as did your immense admiration for de Gaulle. Though you were the bright product of a Marist education, you loathed and detested rugby and the culture that surrounds it; but should a French side be here playing tests against the All Blacks, you would have the radio on loud in the hopes of a victory by the tourists. You were, of course, usually disappointed in this hope.

Your general lack of business sense or, for that matter, interest in business.

Your occasional predilection for collecting junk – those shelves full

NICHOLAS WITH
JOHN REID, 1960

of second-hand science-fiction magazines which you never read, but which you bought up because they were going cheap. The cardboard cut-out fish which you bagged from the decorations at some Arts Ball and then (to my sister's disgust) nailed up in our playroom. Those piles of unplayable (and never-played) 78s which you allowed an old man to make a hobby of buying for you at flea-markets. I think you were good to a number of unloved or eccentric people, like that particular old man, who thought he was rendering you a very important service.

To the irritation of my more practical-minded siblings, you were useless with machines. I remember one Sunday afternoon of your fuming and raging over an uncooperative editing machine as you tried to splice together some home movies. Godfrey used to joke that the local garage lived off servicing and repairing the second-hand bombs you always bought. Certainly you never owned a new car. Miriam wished you wouldn't deliver her each morning up the driveway of her girls' school in a rust-ridden vehicle that backfired. But in your mellower moods you admitted your limitations in this area. I was about 15 when I had inherited the chore of mowing the lawn each week. One Saturday morning, the damned mower just wouldn't start. I had cleaned the spark plugs and checked the petrol flow and yanked and yanked and yanked at the starter until I was swearing. You bustled down the back stairs, irritated at my apparent incompetence, and took over. You yanked and yanked and yanked and got red in the face and swore and yanked some more and finally kicked the machine and gave up with another curse. After this performance, I decided to give it one more try before taking the morning off. I pulled the cord, and the machine came to life at once. You had the spirit to nearly fall down laughing at the cheek of it. I think you actually paid me for my efforts that week.

You knew you weren't good at some things, but at other things you were brilliant. You were a witty lecturer. You were an inspiring teacher. Even allowing for the fact that people will say pleasant things to me (as your son) about you, I have been impressed over the years by the number of those who have said, 'I still remember your father's lectures on *Bleak House.*' Or, 'Your father really turned me on to reading Fielding.' Or, 'I loved the way your father stuck up for the underdog', referring to your championing of literary eccentrics like William Barnes or Thomas Love Peacock. I knew from experiencing them how ready your debating skills always were, how quickly you could come up with a funny phrase or an intriguing reference. But even here the fact of your death cuts me off from really appreciating you. Only once do I remember sitting in on a course of lectures you were giving – a rather plodding series of stage three talks on *King Lear*, all perfectly scholarly and coherent and ordered, but delivered at dictation speed (for which, incidentally, most of your student audience was extremely grateful) and without any particular sparkle. Looking back, I realise this was in the last year of your life, and I also begin to wonder how conscious you were of my presence. I know now how off-putting and constricting that can be. One of my own sons had the misfortune to spend a year in my form seven English class, and I think our discomfort was mutual.

So even for this most public side of you, I am driven back to other people's observations. Of John Reid as lecturer, I recall not something I saw myself, but one of Mum's favourite anecdotes. Apparently you had had a packed lecture theatre cheering and applauding and rolling in the aisles at your jokes in a joyful hullaballoo such as rarely occurred in the halls of learning. The crowd listening to you dispersed, to be replaced by a small group of students for a French lecture. Responding to your performance, the incoming French lecturer remarked, with self-deprecating wit, to his tiny audience, '*Après le déluge, moi.*'

Proudly, Mum would often quote this: '*Après le déluge, moi.*'

Now why, Dad, does this phrase seem so resonant to me?

Since your death, I have found myself sometimes very protective of your academic reputation. I know you had enemies and critics, some of them your enemies for the most discreditable of reasons. As an American sociologist remarked, anti-Catholicism is the anti-Semitism of the intellectuals. Both on campus and off, there was the odd agnostic zealot willing to disparage you on ideological grounds, though I think you gave as good as you got in this area.

Off in a universe of his own making, that old misanthrope Frank Sargeson got paranoid over anything approaching criticism (including your own) of his work. Besides, he had little in common with married heterosexuals who had large families. So he included a caricature of you, Ritchie, in his novel *Memoirs of a Peon*. But the only way he could find to deflate his fictional Ritchie was the melodramatic method of turning the character into a wife-beater. Personally, what I found most offensive about this was the fact that he gave Ritchie a mere six children. You, while aware of the caricature, chose to suavely under-react. Only recently did I discover that in a survey volume of New Zealand literature, you praised *Memoirs of a Peon* as 'a very funny first-person narrative', but mentioned 'its pompous narrator, whose limited self-awareness produces some delicious ironies'.

I'm sure you must have been thinking about Sargeson himself when you wrote that 'limited self-awareness' bit.

More than any other kind, though, your critics were ivory-tower dwellers who thought a man who did so much book and film reviewing, Film Society-organising, theatre fund-raising, and broad-casting (not to mention family-raising) couldn't possibly be an academic heavyweight. Serious academics took a whole year off to produce a slim monograph. Serious academics ferreted away at a narrow specialty and then congratulated themselves on their profundity. They did not spread themselves about or enter the vulgar marketplace of ideas and make public displays of themselves.

There now, Dad. You see how defensive I am about your reputation, even after all these years that you have been lying in a Mangere grave? I try hard to look at your adversaries with an impartial eye (which of course I can never do). I can't remember you yourself ever complaining about criticism, or even taking the slightest notice of adverse comments. You were probably too busy getting on with your next project. In fact, one dinner-table conversation, in which you mildly criticised a colleague's laziness, was the only time I ever heard you say anything negative about another academic. But here I am hammering away at the point as if you, with your choleric self-assurance and wide circle of friends, were somehow a victim. It's really only since your death that I have met your critics – mainly in print, in the odd passing, snide comment – and most of them come up looking pretty small-minded.

But, Dad, neither of us is so myopic as to imagine that all criticism of you was without foundation. With your energy, you could be bumptious and peremptory. With your verbal skills, you could be loudly opinionated. You could out-talk most comers and hold a debating chamber in the palm of your hand. I'm sure at least some of your critics must have been people whom you had verbally worsted, sullenly licking their wounds after public humiliation. Sometimes, as a teenager, I can remember wishing that you did not have the right judgement quite so readily to hand. And on one occasion (just one occasion), I can remember being positively embarrassed by your public self. You were appearing on some commercial radio discussion of pop records (the type of thing you did that was regarded as disgustingly lowbrow and vulgar by your more prim colleagues). Listening in at home, I heard some barely articulate rocker mumble his suggestion that the latest banal release was 'the music of the people'. Whereupon you, with crushing articulateness, verbally stomped all over the poor mug, leaving him with nothing to say for the rest of the show.

I wish you hadn't done that, Dad. Maybe you had had a hard week, but it really was a contest of unequals. Heavy artillery against a pea-shooter. One of those times when your wit and confidence curdled into intellectual bullying and verbal brow-beating.

Yet, as with machines, so with your verbal display. You knew when you were in the wrong, when you had gone too far, when inspiring words became domineering, dogmatic verbiage. Here is my last clear memory of you before seeing your face (unreally powdered and painted) in the funeral parlour. You were in hospital, after the first major tremor, and before the big heart attack that killed you. I happened to be the only visitor in your room for an hour or so – that in itself was a small miracle, given that your extended family and colleagues and the bishop and the rabbi and Mercury Theatre actors were trooping up to pay their respects. I've always found it very hard to make sickbed conversation, so I decided to give you a performance instead. I had just been downtown watching Monty Python's *And Now For Something Completely Different*, so I gave you my version of the then-new 'Lumberjack Song' and the 'Who's a Fairy in the Army?' routine ('Squadron – camp it – UP!'). You laughed hard enough for me to wonder if I hadn't chosen the wrong material for somebody who was still, after all, attached to life-support systems. Then you calmed down and said philosophically, 'Oh well, I suppose I'll be back home in a few days, shouting and grumbling and giving orders'.

I never knew you more peaceful and resigned than in that sad admission, and I knew that, faced with death, you were apologising for some haste and rage and the occasional verbal stomping.

I cannot consider you at all without considering this whole public side of you. Since your death, it is where I have met you most often. But this letter is supposed to be about you and me, what you gave to me and how I responded to you. And I now have the self-conscious task of drawing out what exactly you put into my heart and head.

Most important were one thing unintended, and three healthy lessons. The one thing unintended first.

You gave me a mountain of unexamined opinions. I do not mean they were unexamined by you. I mean they were unexamined by me. As a little boy and an adolescent, I heard from you (in talk at the dinner table or on evening strolls or Sunday spins) many things clearly expressed about art and literature and politics and religion and life. You did not usually lecture when you conversed, but much was conveyed in the by-the-way comment here and the parenthesis there. I realised quite early that I could pass for an educated and well-read chap simply by repeating the things you had said. As a teenager, this gave me some short-term advantages. But the time always came when I had to separate you from me, and admit that I was using someone else's thinking. What made this process difficult was that your judgements were usually sane and reasonable ones. Often, after putting your view to the test, I found myself in very much the same place I had started from. For example, I knew that D. H. Lawrence had an untenable view of life before I had ever read a scrap of the man's writings. This was because of the odd, offhanded comment you had made on the subject, and your relish in once telling the tale of the esteemed Irish Lawrentian scholar whom you had witnessed in his cups cheerfully admitting, 'Sure, the bugger was mad'. Only years later did I read my way through Lawrence's works, and I discovered how right you were.

Of course, a counter-thought intrudes at this point. Would I have come to this conclusion if I had not been cued to it? At the age of 45, I think I have figured out my own views on many things, but in my lazier moments it may be J. C. Reid who is doing my thinking for me. All of which is, of course, merely an elaborate way of admitting that I am my father's son.

I am less troubled by the three healthy lessons that your whole life taught. The first, and most paradoxical, was the sense you always gave that the arts and literature, and especially literary criticism, were in themselves not the most important things in life. You enjoyed opera and music and film and you opened many doors that allowed me to enjoy these things too. You reverenced some great writers; you were a genuine enthusiast for many books; and your own critical standards were high. But you never led me to believe that these things were life itself, or were as important as the really essential things – family, fun, religion, goodness to others, the well-being of society. In the end, as you constantly implied, criticism is a game, an intriguing and complex game, perhaps, but a game nevertheless; and if there is no delight in it, then it is not worth playing.

I think you would have approved when, a few years after your death, your friend and colleague Mike Joseph told a reporter that university humanities departments were 'basically in the entertainment business'. Nowadays, his attitude, like your own, would be guaranteed to enrage earnest fools engaged in semiotic deconstructions, structuralist (and post-structuralist) analyses, post-modernist discourses (always on 'texts'), radical-feminist contextualisations. The more earnest the critic, the more the poor devil is probably trying to turn literature into what it can never be – a touchstone of ultimate values or a substitute for the certainties of religion.

You honoured real scholarship, but you were as aware as any sane person must be that real scholarship does not always happen in tertiary institutions, and much that appears in print beneath academic names is merely part of the great publish-or-perish game of tenure-seekers.

I have just put into your dead mouth opinions that I never heard you express in so many words. But I deduce them from the hilarity you often expressed over really pretentious pieces of academic writing, from your constant willingness to parody obscure and self-important criticism, and from your pleasure in addressing the wider community outside the campus and the common room. And I know you enjoyed the gentle wit of Beachcomber's satire on obsessive academics, 'Professor Strabismus (whom God preserve) of Utrecht'.

The second lesson your life taught me was intimately related to the first. This was your deep pleasure in, and healthy respect for, cultural vulgarity. You had a fund of music-hall songs (to go with your fund of Gilbert and Sullivan patter) which you could recite on demand. You knew, verbatim, vaudeville comedy routines and catch-phrases which you had picked up in your youth, and you would burst out at odd moments with phrases such as 'What a common office boy!' or 'It's being so cheerful as keeps me going', or you would hum the theme to *Much Binding in the Marsh*. I remember your belly-laughs when you first read Flann O'Brien's *The Third Policeman*, and I must admit it still figures on my own list of The 10 Most Enjoyable Books of All Time. ITMA ('It's That Man Again'), the Goons, the Marx Brothers, the young Ealing Studio's Alec Guinness – you loved them all. Before they demolished the old Mayfair cinema in Auckland, I can remember how you would take us along in the school holidays to see the double features they used to screen of (already ancient) Laurel and Hardy and Marx Brothers flicks. Stan and Ollie getting the whole regiment to walk in step with them in *Bonnie Scotland*, or playing the earsie-nosie game in *Fra Diavolo*, or performing some ritual retaliation on a berserk James Finlayson; I think of these things and I think of you roaring at them. Thanks to the invention of the video-recorder, I have passed on the faith. My older children never did take to Laurel and Hardy, but they are pretty good at imitating Groucho doing the 'Land of the Free' number from *Duck Soup*, or working out the legal contract with Chico in *A Night at the Opera*.

I have never shared your taste for detective novels, but I remember how you would bring a satchel of them home from the Auckland Central Library one Monday night, and have them all read by the next, because you had the ability to read a whole light thriller in the half-hour between going to bed and turning out the light. 'Defective novels' you jocularly called them, and for many years that is what I thought they were properly called.

Then there were comics. When we were kids you arranged, for three or four years, for bundles of *Beano* and *Dandy* and *Eagle* to be mailed directly to us from their British publishers. We thought this was very generous of you, but we did notice that you always got to read the comics first – especially the adventures of Desperate Dan. I suspect the same was true of the Tintin books that regularly found their way into our pillow-cases at Christmas.

Had Professor Pooter or Professor Prim Spinster or Professor Agnostic Zealot or Professor Pretentious even heard of Groucho and Chico and Stan and Ollie and Captain Haddock and Dan Dare and Eccles and the lugubrious Tony Hancock with his tuba intro? Somehow I doubt it. Yet I wonder how you would have reacted to the dead hand of Academe now falling on popular culture, with the growth industry in film studies and media studies that has happened since your death? On the whole, I don't think you would have approved.

As for the third implicit lesson – it has to do with this whole Catholic thing. Not by words, but by your whole example, you taught that the Church is not to be confused with its clergy. This lesson began quite early in my life. Coming home from convent school at the age of seven or eight, I repeated the Irish sister's insistence that the Pope was 'Eye-talian'. You unobtrusively corrected my pronunciation, but I quickly got the message – Sister did not have all the answers and Sister was not always right because (if it came to a dispute over pronunciation) you were obviously more right than she was. I think trendy seminarians would say we were 'doing' contextual theology in working out these relationships. Later, there was the cocky Doctor of Divinity from Rome who substituted for the parish priest for a couple of months. He used to fill his sermons with quotations from Dante and the *Summa* in the original, which had parishioners scratching their heads and wondering where this stuff was in their missals. You were scathing about him, which immediately taught me another lesson – Father didn't have all the answers either. So it went on over the years, like a measured dose of vaccine. The result is that I have never been particularly scandalised by the shortcomings of the clergy, because I was never trained to see them as paragons in the first place.

Sometimes I have met Father Scholarly, Father Modest, Father Sensible, Father Inspiring, and Father Saintly. But just as often I have met Father Smug, Father Pompous, Father Fatgut, Father Vacuous, Father Naive, Father Mummy's Boy, and even Father Pervert, and they haven't yet succeeded in driving me from the fold. Recently, I read a book of interviews with New Zealand men who had had a Catholic upbringing. I found it quite disconcerting that so many of them claimed they were taught to tug the forelock at all priests. This never was your style. In fact, given that you were conservative in a number of your views, I think many of your co-religionists would have been surprised that you privately described yourself as 'a Catholic anti-clerical'. I knew what you meant. Priests are the uniformed foot-soldiers of the church, licensed to do one very important task, namely, to say Mass. They are not popes, oracles or the Magisterium itself, and really they should know their place in the order of things.

I admit here that there was another Catholic attitude that you passed on to me. Come Sunday morning you would often grumble, complain, and be in an ill humour before going to Mass. But muttering as you did so, you still went and did your duty to God. This, I think, contrasts with the idea that religion is essentially a matter of internals and conscientious disposition (an attitude which easily degenerates into Goethe's *'Gefühl ist alles'* [Feeling is all]). Religion has its externals as well as its internals, and we should pay attention to both. At least, this is the sacramental thought I console myself with on Sunday mornings, as I help Gabrielle buckle squealing younger children into our rust-ridden van and set off for church, whingeing about the banal nature of modern liturgy.

'Remember me when I am dead / and simplify me when I'm dead.' How serviceable and true Keith Douglas' lines still are! I'm aware that even in picking over the word 'Catholic' I am provoking assumptions (or prejudices) in readers of this letter. Recently, a book of teenage reminiscences was published by the son of the old pal with whom you sometimes (amateurishly) played golf on Saturday mornings. The memoirist makes a few passing references to you, mainly friendly (a paragraph on John Reid filling his pipe, etc.). But he does also refer to 'Professor Reid's Index of Forbidden Books', as if he can make an automatic equation of your Catholicism with literary censorship.

Index of Forbidden Books? I know how (small 'c') catholic your reading habits really were. Didn't you take pleasure in discovering and promoting genuine literary oddballs, regardless of how little you agreed with their views? Well do I remember twice, as a teenager, being alone at home when a roaring drunk Ronald Hugh Morrieson rang to earnestly solicit your opinion on something, you having been the person who had recommended his first books for publication (though, I note, others have subsequently attempted to take the credit for this).

I seem to recall that you were the chap who crossed swords with more conservative Catholics (Pat Lawlor et al.) over the right of school-kids to read *The Catcher in the Rye*, the whisky-priest novel of Graham Greene, and so on. When I was 12 or 13, I checked out from the local library a copy of James Joyce's *Portrait of the Artist as a Young Man*. I came home, seated myself in an armchair in the living room, and ostentatiously began to read. Mum caught sight of the book's title and fluttered in agitation through to your study. I heard her say to you, 'He's got *Portrait of the Artist as a Young Man*'. I regret that I did not hear the exact words you said in reply to her, but I heard your tone of voice as you half-whispered a reply. It was conciliatory, and I took the tone to mean something like 'Oh well. It's a good book. I hope he enjoys it.' So I continued to read undisturbed.

Actually, Dad, at that age I had the habit of starting grown-up books but giving up on them after a few pages. I'm sorry that I followed the self-absorbed Stephen Dedalus for only about 20 pages that time; but *Portrait* turned up as our set text at Sacred Heart College four years later. Good book, too. It helps to explain why Jimmy Joyce ended up playing word-games.

The mention of Joyce reminds me of a spotty young seminarian who was once present at a combined family picnic. He spent the whole day tagging about after you whining out such questions as 'Doctor Reid, would it be a sin to read James Joyce?' Finally, in exasperation, you turned on him and robustly replied, 'In your case, I think it would be a sin if you *didn't* read James Joyce.'

Quite so.

Cultural attitudes and healthy vulgarity and Catholicism – if that were all you gave me, it would be a narrow, theoretical and depressingly cerebral list. But attitudes and intentional teachings are only a small part of being a father. How good a father were you to me? It is almost impossible for me to answer that question. Against what (or whom) would I be measuring you? As you are the only father I ever had, the very concept of fatherliness brings an image of you to my mind. You have become for me an absolute value, and absolute values aren't open to comparison. But if I tried really hard, I could manufacture an artificial indignation over how busy and preoccupied you sometimes were during my adolescence. It was Mum, rather than you, who would turn up to see me in school plays or concerts. You would most likely be out somewhere giving a lecture or talk. When I was 17, I bagged the lead role in the school production; but you never did see me, with my white beard, bidding the winds blow and crack their cheeks, because you were on sabbatical leave in Europe at the time. If I added soundtrack music to this circumstance, I could easily work it up into a piece of self-pitying teen angst along Hollywood lines (*The Breakfast Club*, *Dead Poets Society*, or some such). In fact, at the time I don't remember being particularly distressed, as your not being available in the evenings was something I took for granted. Weren't you the man who once changed Guy Fawkes Night to 4 November, so that you could personally supervise our rocket-shooting, as you had to be out on the night itself?

Besides, I know you tried very hard to balance your family and your public career. Even as you worked, you wanted to be involved with us. Visitors to our home sometimes expressed surprise that your study was separated from our main living room only by a small and incomplete wooden partition. Your typewriter clacking away was often the background to our playing board games, chatting or watching television. There you would be typing away and smoking your pipe, and there we would be chattering; and then a comment of yours would fly across the partition and we would realise that you were following what we were saying even as you worked. This sort of intervention could be funny and it could be embarrassing. As a 13-year-old, I was reduced to paroxysms of helpless giggling, as were the schoolmates I was entertaining, when the loud, explosive sound of your fart resounded over the partition, followed by your meek 'Pardon!'. Later, you would sometimes add comments or footnotes to my attempts at intellectual discussion with student friends. Two of my mates at the time became adept at mimicking you dashing out from your study with a reference book when our conversation had stalled over some point of fact and you wanted to set us straight. Needless to add, we sometimes decamped to another part of the house when we really wanted to let rip.

Aware as I am that you had six other children, and that your universe did not revolve around me, I think you tried to show no favouritism to any of us. When you and Mum came back from your last sabbatical, 17-year-old me and 19-year-old Godfrey went down to Wellington to meet you. We all drove back up to Auckland together. On the journey, I realised you weren't letting either of us hog the conversation. You would ask me a question about arty-farty matters and then Godfrey a question about the air force; me a question about my last exams, and then him a question about gliding. So it went on until we reached the hotel in Putaruru, where we stayed for the night. Even at the time, I could see your strategy. You were telling us that neither of us was more or less important than the other. I saw and understood that it was both obvious and right.

We have to admit that you did have a temper. You did sometimes fly into rages. I did sometimes feel the back of your hand. Living just up the little rise from us, Ron Holloway's family nicknamed you 'Froggy', because some quiet nights, if the wind was right, they could hear you bellowing like a bullfrog and us squeaking and scampering like your froglings.

But I can't remember your interventions or your outbursts dom-inating our lives, and I can't make them the measure of your fatherhood. In this matter I speak partly from self-interest. I have children of my own, and I would hate them to judge me by what is worst in me. Five years back, Gabrielle and I were going to take our first summer holiday ever without our children. We were leaving three teenagers in charge of an 11-year-old and a six-year-old. As we were about to exit, I began to fuss and worry over how they would get on for five days without us. Whereupon my eldest son said, 'Don't worry, Dad, I can do everything you do.' He proceeded to run upstairs, seat himself at my desk, and give a very good impression of me shouting, 'Could you damned kids be quiet down there?'

When it comes to child-rearing, I know my children could reproach me for the same things I could hold against you, and this fact does get into perspective any lingering teenage grievances I may still harbour. In this respect, I have become very suspicious of demolitions of parents written by childless authors, like Samuel Butler spending a lifetime whining about his clergyman father. Such people haven't seen the clouds from both sides and don't know how peripheral (from an adult's perspective) can be those things that children think are of the utmost importance. The culture of complaint; the culture of aggrieved adolescence carried into middle age; 'Daddy Dearest', 'Mommie Dearest': it would all be blown away by the exercise of parenthood. I am delighted that my eldest son used to laugh before he did his impression of James Dean, in *Rebel Without a Cause*, clutching his head and groaning at his parents, 'You're tearing me apart!' At least he understood that such images of adolescent anxiety (see any soap opera) are as much media constructs as are thriller supermen immune to bullets. They have little to do with the dynamics of real families.

Which brings me to my own major artificial construct in writing this letter. Trying to assess you alone as a parent ignores the fact that Mum was always at your side, that your first loyalty was to her, and that any effect you had as a parent was harnessed to the effect she was having – your religious polemic matched by her religious piety; your worst moments of pomposity deflated by her irony and common sense (her 'Go boil your head!' is still a delicious phrase to me); your abstractions and large gestures no more important than her specific anecdotes. A few years back, I found I had developed the habit of facetiously adding the phrase 'as my old mother used to say' to anything self-evidently true that I had to say. Then I reflected that the phrase itself was no less than the literal truth. Really intimate household wisdom was Mum's to impart, not yours. It was she, not you, who would read to us Browning's 'Pied Piper' and Hardy's 'Weathers' and Kipling's 'The Way Through the Wood'. And it was she, not you, who would happily tell us stories about your youth and early married life. What I am saying is that it was left to her (and maybe Uncle Dave) after your death to tell us about your own poverty-wracked childhood; your road labourer father and the moonlight flits he had to arrange ahead of the rent man; your epileptic stepmother and all the other things you were too personally modest to talk about. There was a whole side of you I did not know when you were alive; and it is left to me to point out the irony of your having dirt under your fingernails while some of the lefty-liberal antagonists of your youth hailed from comfy bourgeois addresses.

When I began thinking about this letter, I vaguely remembered your obituary in the *Listener*, and I seemed to recall that it was a little patronising. There was a phrase in which the writer declared, 'the John Reid I knew was a good deal more tolerant . . . than the young John Reid had been', which sounded like a backhanded compliment at best.

It rankled. So I dug through yellowing memorabilia and looked again at the obituary for the first time in 25 years. Expecting to take the writer to task for his attitude, I instead found that Dennis McEldowney had been very positive about you and generous to a fault. The simple fact is that my memory (or maybe my tender perceptions at the age of 20) had been in error.

I had misremembered.

This whole letter has been memory – my fallible and porous memory. If Christopher or Bernard or Piers or Gerard or Miriam or Godfrey were to write about you, then their fallible memories would surely come up with something radically different from mine. Each observed you for a different length of your time line, and from a different angle. We do not have you to compare our memories with, and we cannot produce a definitive version of you.

In the end, Dad, this is the worst thing I can say about you as a parent. You are dead. I have lived more of my life without you than with you, but a big part of me is still unreconciled to this fact.

Hoping to meet you again somehow,

Your son,
Nicholas

SNAPSHOTS OF MY FATHER

HARRY RICKETTS on *JOHN RICKETTS*

I

After my father died in 1992, my mother was flooded with letters of condolence. At his memorial service in Worcester Cathedral, over 500 people came to pay their last respects. As I stood at the lectern, reading the passage from *Pilgrim's Progress* where Mr. Valiant-for-Truth 'passed over, and all the trumpets sounded for him on the other side', I remember thinking that it had never occurred to me that so many people valued my father so highly. But they obviously did because they all wrote or spoke so glowingly of him: 'John was always such a gentleman'; 'Your father was a truly good man'; 'He was a Christian soldier'. It wasn't that I didn't recognise my father in these eulogies; it was just that I wasn't used to thinking of him in that way.

What my father's death also brought home to me was that, although a key figure in my life, I never really knew him very well. This was partly the usual consequence of 10 years of English boarding schools: prep school at eight, public school at 13, going home only during the holidays. This kind of separation doesn't tend to encourage intimate relations with your parents, at least, it didn't in my case. In addition, my father was a reticent, self-contained person who seldom discussed his own life and was quickly made uncomfortable by confessional conversations and large displays of emotion. The result is that I never knew that much about him and now tend to think of him in a series of memory-snapshots, usually with a date and place attached.

II

My earliest memory, for instance, is of my father crouching down in the kitchen of our house in Epsom, painting the inside of the back door a pale, duck-egg blue. That must have been in 1953 when I was three, shortly after we had come back from Malaya. In another memory from the same period he is holding me by the ankles and shaking out a threepenny bit I've put in my mouth and half-swallowed. In later memories, between the ages of six and eight, he often appears in uniform with our liver-and-white springer-spaniel trotting at his heels.

He appears in uniform because he was a British Army officer, though unlike several of his army friends he didn't come from a military family. His parents were, in fact, both schoolteachers in the Tewkesbury area of Gloucestershire, which is where my father was born in 1915. Grand-father died in the Spanish flu epidemic shortly after the First World War, and my father, christened Jack, his elder brother Harry, and younger sister Mary were brought up by their mother (my Grandma). After boarding school, my father and Uncle Harry were encouraged to go into the army, my father duly joining the Worcestershire Regiment and my uncle the Leicesters.

I think it was Aunt Mary who told me that even before my father went to Sandhurst as a cadet, he was quietly informed that Jack was a sailor's name and that he'd better change it to John if he wanted to fit in as a soldier. Whether that's true or not, Jack and not John was his real name, though only my aunt and some of his cousins ever used it; everyone else, including my mother, who didn't meet him until he had already been in the army for some years, always called him John. To me, Jack seems a warmer name than John, and I rather regret that my father gave up his original name. At the same time I can see how it might have happened (he always hated fuss) and even how, in a way, John may have been more appropriate for the sort of person he became. When I was a child, I called him 'Dad' or 'Daddy', but when I got older, I switched to the more formal 'Father', and that's still how I think of him.

He retired from the army as a lieutenant-colonel in 1960 after 25 years' service, to become secretary to his old regiment and also, though I was largely unaware of this, came to play a distinguished role in local affairs. In the village outside Worcester where my parents settled down, he was always known as 'the Colonel'. This title, which I think he quite

HARRY WITH
JOHN RICKETTS

enjoyed, perhaps conjures up the image of a Colonel Blimp, someone with a walrus moustache, a barking voice and nothing much between the ears. My father wasn't like that at all. He did have a moustache, it's true, but kept it very closely trimmed and certainly never twirled or stroked it. Nor did he ever bark or talk about tiffin or *chota pegs*, though he had served in India as a young subaltern. He was an essentially quiet person, patient, determined, and so modest that I didn't know until I read his obituary in the *Daily Telegraph* that towards the end of the Second World War he had won a small battle not far from Düsseldorf and been awarded an 'immediate DSO'. His citation, quoted at length in the obituary, concluded: 'He was absolutely fearless and at the crisis of the battle accepted great responsibility. Without previous experience he commanded a battalion and led them through a most difficult attack. His conduct was of the highest order.'

Looking back, it seems characteristic I never heard anything of this from him: that would have been 'swanking', as he might have put it. I do vaguely remember a couple of stories he told me about doing patrols in the Malayan jungle in the early 1950s, but neither concerned heroics: the first was about his corporal climbing up a tree to attach an aerial for the radio and, to general panic and confusion, disturbing a hornets' nest; the other was about laying an ambush for communist guerrillas and how tense he had felt as they waited in hiding hour after hour.

III

That my father was a professional soldier affected my life right from the start. It meant boarding school, for instance, so that my education wouldn't be too disrupted by overseas postings. More particularly, it meant that when I was born, he put my name down for Wellington College, a public school in Berkshire which offered greatly reduced fees for the sons of officers killed on active service; so had my father been killed in the Malayan jungle, as he might well have been, the cost of my education would have been largely covered. Being born into the army meant that, until I was 10, we moved every two or three years, and this imprinted an unconscious pattern which I later repeated for a decade after leaving university: when I'd been teaching somewhere for a few years, I would get restless and apply for a new position, even move to a new country. My father's career also led to my developing very mixed feelings about the army itself which, amongst other things, has fuelled a lifelong fascination with Rudyard Kipling and his work.

Kipling, I'm sure, would have approved of my father, recognising in him the kind of dutiful, hard-working officer he had come to admire as a young journalist in India and whom he had then more or less invented as a literary type. There's an irony in this because my father, far from returning this hypothetical admiration, didn't care for Kipling at all, finding his books much too literary. I suspect he may also have thought (or heard) that some of Kipling wasn't 'quite the thing', to use one of his characteristic understatements. A story like '"Love-o'-Women"', for instance, about a syphilitic gentleman-ranker would have put him off; so too, if he knew of it, would 'Mary Postgate', a study of warped sexual gratification. I know that when he told me that a book of mine about expatriate life in Hong Kong wasn't really his cup of tea (his own phrase), I took him to mean that the stories and poems had too much sex in them. What he liked reading was military history and historical novels, though he also enjoyed the occasional thriller. I imagine he would have considered the very idea of a book like this in which sons write about their fathers 'a bit off'; and had I mentioned that I was going to write about him, I think he would have felt surprised and embarrassed. 'Why on earth would you want to do that?' I can hear him ask in a puzzled voice. I can't imagine he would have read this piece.

IV

Throughout my childhood and most of my teens, the great tie between my father and me was cricket. A photograph, taken when

I was five, shows me in shirt, sandals and shorts, swinging a cricket bat with fierce determination. Apparently, that same summer, I also used to run round and round the tiny lawn in the back garden, whirling my arms and shouting: 'I'm Typhoon Tyson!' The thing was, I knew that I could always get my father's attention if I suggested cricket. For him it provided a ready-made means of doing something with me, of establishing a bond, without the need for much talking. He could say the occasional 'Good shot' or 'Well bowled' or 'Try again', and that was all that was required by way of conversation.

His patience was extraordinary. From the age of 11 to 15, most dry evenings of the Easter and summer holidays, I would be eagerly waiting for him when he got home from work. He was allowed a quick cup of tea and a piece of cake, and then I expected an hour or two's cricket on the lawn (a larger one now, the size of a reasonable tennis court). Mostly he bowled at me, over after over of slow left-arm spin, with our dog Shot fielding at cover point and retrieving the ball which became increasingly slobbery and hard to hold. Less frequently he would bat, right-handed, correct, careful not to endanger the French windows. Then one evening when I was 13 and able to bowl a bit quicker, I hit him on the shoulder; after that, when he wasn't bowling or giving me fielding practice, he would act as umpire and encourage me to aim at the stumps.

Cricket also solved the problem of joint excursions with my father. We were members of the Worcestershire County Cricket Club, and in the summer holidays he and I would often go down to watch my heroes, especially the elegant Tom Graveney, of whom it used to be said that he didn't so much hit the ball as 'persuade it to the boundary'. I remember us watching the first day of Worcestershire's game against the 1961 Australians, an April day of intense nervous excitement as far as I was concerned. After the great Australians (Harvey, O'Neill, Benaud) had miraculously been bundled out for 177, Worcestershire lost some quick wickets before Graveney came in and stayed until stumps. To me, it looked as though my hero was being pretty lucky, and in my anxiety I asked my father why he kept playing and missing so much outside the off-stump. It was all right, my father reassured me, Graveney wasn't really playing and missing; he was aiming his shots well away from the ball; and he was doing this quite deliberately so as to accustom himself to the pace and bounce of the pitch. Gosh, I thought, deeply impressed, what a player! Looking back, I can't decide whether my father believed his own explanation or whether, seeing my anxiety, he was simply trying to cheer me up. But at the time I know I was utterly convinced of Graveney's superior batting technique and of my father's superior cricketing knowledge.

My father and I only ever played against each other in a match on three occasions: twice in the annual fathers and sons' match at my prep school and once in my late teens. On none of these occasions did either of us succeed in getting the other out though we both tried hard enough, and my father bowled at me much faster than he ever did at home in the garden. During the tea interval of the second of these matches, after he had finished a longish spell and was feeling that he had acquitted himself quite well, a junior boy came up and asked him: 'Sir, were you a real fast bowler in your prime?' He was very tickled by this question, and for the next few months it became a running family joke. Even after we finally stopped those evening sessions on the lawn, my father continued to take a keen interest in my cricket, and I think the moment he was proudest of me was when I rang to tell him that I had been awarded my First XI colours.

V

Outside playing, watching or talking cricket, my father and I didn't begin to communicate very successfully until I got married in my late twenties and had a family of my own. I've often thought that part of our awkwardness with each other was because, like many Englishmen of his background and generation, he was more at ease with animals than with children. I don't mean that he loved the three dogs we had more than he loved me, simply that he didn't know how to express his love for me except by being utterly reliable – a quality it took me many years to come to value, though I did in the end. Even as a child, I could dimly sense that he was somehow more spontaneously affectionate with our dogs than with me. 'You old rascal' or 'You old rogue', he would say in an especially gentle voice, ruffling their ears or giving them a hearty pat; they in turn were devoted to him.

The first of these dogs came to live with us in 1955 soon after we moved from Epsom to Norton Barracks on the outskirts of Worcester. My father heard of a local gamekeeper who had an ageing liver-and-white springer he wanted to get rid of and, liking the idea of owning a trained gun-dog, my father decided to take him. Gay, as the springer was inappropriately called – he had the most mournful expression you ever saw – had led a fairly hard life and wasn't at all used to being indoors. This became clear as soon as we brought him home and took him into the kitchen where he promptly cocked his leg against the kitchen-table, much to my delight.

Gay's devotion to my father soon became a byword around the barracks: he used to follow my father everywhere, even on to the parade-ground. But though he quickly became house-trained, Gay never entirely lost the air of being slightly disreputable, and I think my father, who was very proper himself, derived a certain vicarious enjoyment from Gay's occasional waywardness.

One instance of this occurred during Regimental Cricket Week. One morning shortly before the start of play, my father, still in his everyday clothes, strolled out towards the middle to say hello to Major Hunter who took his cricket very seriously and had been carefully inspecting the wicket. Cricket was not the only thing Major Hunter took seriously; he also took immense pains with his turn-out, hence his regimental nickname of 'Gentleman Jim'. That morning he was immaculate in blazer and perfectly ironed and creased white flannels. Gay, who as usual was trotting behind my father, obviously didn't think much of Gentleman Jim's sartorial pretensions because he went straight up to the perfectly ironed and creased white flannels and very deliberately peed all over them, in full view of a large number of spectators. At the time it must have been mortifying for my father, but at some level he must also have enjoyed it because I later heard him tell the story several times, chuckling as he did so. Shot, the mongrel that followed Gay, never quite matched his instinct for low comedy, but she had great intelligence and a very sweet nature, and I remember my mother telling me that when she died, my father cried as he buried her in the garden. Donna, his last dog, had previously belonged to one of his closest friends, and when she developed cancer and had to be put down, he decided enough was enough.

VI

Though not a great conversationalist, on subjects which mattered to him my father usually talked good sense. We often disagreed, but I came to respect the fact that he rarely said things just for the sake of argument.

As I've already implied, sex was an uncomfortable topic, and our 'sex talk' was a model of its kind. My father and I were in the car one day, driving towards Worcester in companionable silence; I must have been about 13. Suddenly, out of the blue, looking straight ahead through the windscreen, he asked rather awkwardly: 'Is there anything you want to know? You know, about . . .' His voice trailed off. Something about his tone supplied the missing word. At that age the depth of my ignorance about sex was as limitless as my curiosity. There were so many things I wanted to ask. Really basic things. What did you do exactly? What was it like? Would I ever do it? Did wanking really make you go blind? What did girls have 'down there'? As these and similar questions flooded my mind, I realised that I couldn't possibly ask my father any of them. 'No, nothing,' I said, also looking straight ahead, and we continued towards Worcester in relieved silence.

Private or personal subjects in general were better avoided, and he seldom brought up the past. Perhaps he didn't think about it much; it's hard to know. So the conversation we had about Uncle Harry's death, when I was back in England on a visit in the mid-1980s, stands out with distinct clarity. We were driving back to Worcester from Cirencester. I had been invited to lunch by two members of the Kipling Society and, to save me taking the train, my father had offered to drive me over. One of our hosts, it turned out, remembered meeting my uncle at a hotel in Cornwall in the 1930s and, what was more, produced a photograph of him. On the return journey, my father told me about my uncle's death. I had always been curious about Uncle Harry because I knew that I was his namesake, a decision apparently imposed on my parents by Grandma. I also knew vaguely what had happened to him – that he had died in the Second World War in unfortunate circumstances – but the details were pretty hazy.

What actually happened was this. Uncle Harry was captured by the Germans in North Africa and sent across with a boatload of other prisoners to a POW camp in northern Italy. When Italy surrendered in

1943, he and the other POWs were let out and faced a choice of either making their way north to Switzerland or heading south towards the Allied advance. Uncle Harry and a couple of others slowly worked their way south, hiding out in the hills and receiving food and help from local farmers. (For a decade after the war, Grandma used to send boots to one particular family who had harboured Harry.) But when they eventually reached the Allied lines, one of the group trod on an Allied mine and they were blown up. My uncle died a few days later in a field hospital. My father told the story in his usual voice without any special emphasis though as far as I know he had been fond of his brother, who was a large, jolly man and the family extrovert.

VII

Like all very self-controlled people, when my father lost his temper, he lost it quite dramatically. I remember, for instance, his rage when Grandma died. He and my mother were then living in Hong Kong where he was commanding the Hong Kong Regiment, his last posting before he retired. It was 1958, and I had flown over for the summer holidays after my first term at prep school. He was in a rage for three days, almost unrecognisable as my father, and though his rage wasn't directed at me, I found it absolutely terrifying, and bewildering. On the few occasions I had met her, Grandma had struck me as an alarming figure: she suffered from cataracts and used to stare at me through a magnifying glass which made one eye look enormous. As a result, I thought of her as a kind of witch. It wasn't until years later that it occurred to me my father's rage was really grief, probably exacerbated by guilt that he wasn't there when she died. He flew over to England for the funeral and when he returned, he was my father again.

As a teenager, I sometimes used to bait my father to see if I could make him lose his temper. This was the period of my life, from approximately 15 to 18, when I needed him to be the epitome of everything I considered boring, unimaginative and reactionary. My favourite book at this time was Forster's *Howards End*, in which people are conveniently divided up into Schlegels ('the passion') and Wilcoxes ('the prose'). Since in my own mind I was obviously a Schlegel, my father was obviously a Wilcox and therefore fair game for anything I cared to dish out. So I would bring up topical issues like the death penalty or immigration or homosexuality – any issue on which I guessed he would have conservative views – knowing that eventually I would be able to provoke him into some outburst which he would later regret.

With my own children and stepchildren, he was almost unfailingly patient and kind, though I'm sure he found them more rewarding once they were old enough to play cards or catch or be taken for walks. The only occasion I can recall him losing his temper with one of them was with my three-year-old daughter, Jess. My parents' house had some nice furniture and porcelain in it and it wasn't exactly child-proof. One day, the morning we were to leave after a short stay, my daughter touched something delicate, and my father exploded at her. A week or so later, a letter arrived, full of apologies and saying how ashamed he felt about his behaviour.

VIII

It was having children that brought me closer to my father. Though I had more or less grown out of trying to bait him by the time I left school, it took me a lot longer to give up my image of him as dully decent; and then for a time it suited me, on and off, to see him as something more melodramatic. For most of my student years and into my mid-twenties, I fervently wanted to believe in those two great slogans of arrested adolescence: Wilde's 'Children begin by loving their parents; after a time they judge them; rarely, if ever, do they forgive them' and Larkin's 'They fuck you up, your mum and dad'. I took it for granted that my friends and I were all in some way 'fucked up' and that in my case the blame lay with my father who patently didn't understand me and who had sent me off to boarding school at the age of eight. I had to make the most of my 'abandonment' at boarding school because, as I was even then dimly aware, I didn't have much else to complain about. My father might be reticent, unbookish and rather narrow in his views, but that was all; he had never mistreated or bullied or abused me. It seems to me now that, perversely, what I really resented was having had such a normal, untraumatic childhood, which meant that whatever problems I had were largely self-generated or going to happen anyway.

Much easier to see my problems as the fault of my parents and particularly my father. And was I going to forgive him? Of course not. My myth of myself was that I was a writer, or going to be one, and I knew that you couldn't be a real writer unless you had a damaged childhood. So in every way it suited me to make my father responsible. But when later I had children myself and started to appreciate some of the difficulties of being a parent, I quite soon got around to forgiving my father. Or to put it more accurately, I came to see that, in fact, there was not a lot that needed forgiving.

IX

Though for a time it was convenient for me to see him as a Wilcox, my father did possess a more dashing, more romantic side, but this, like much else, was usually kept under wraps. As a career, the army probably most satisfies those who desire a life of adventure and discipline, of action within ordered limits. That at least seems to have been the case with my father; and as he wasn't naturally flamboyant and I obviously never saw him 'in action', I only caught occasional hints of this other side of him. For instance, I remember him telling me towards the end of his life that for five or six years after he retired from the Army, he found it extremely hard to accept that there would be no more postings, that he was going to have to settle down. At the time of course I had no inkling of this restlessness, but suppressed wanderlust perhaps explains his delight in airports. Over the years, being delivered or collected, I spent a lot of time with him at airports, and it was evident that he loved watching the planes land and take off and enjoyed speculating about where they had come from or were going to. 'I wonder if that one's from Basra,' he might say. Or, 'I expect that one's off to Singapore.'

I suspect that his pleasure in historical novels was in part a reflection of this subdued romantic streak, as was his liking for historical films. I remember that during one of my visits in the 1980s, the BBC was running a late-night Greta Garbo season which I was eager to catch. *Queen Christina* had just begun when my father, in pyjamas and dressing-gown, opened the study door to say goodnight. Seeing something was 'on the box', he came in without a word, sat down and started watching too. After half an hour or so, he suddenly remarked: 'I saw this as a cadet 50 years ago at Sandhurst'. And when an hour later the film finished, he said, 'I enjoyed seeing that again', and went off to bed. This little episode is amongst my favourite memories of my father.

To others, this more romantic side was probably more self-evident. I can still recall my mild surprise (around the age of 20) when a friend's mother took to referring to my father as 'David Niven'. And my mother has often told me that she more or less fell in love with my father at first sight; she was then a 17-year-old schoolgirl, and he a 27-year-old lieutenant.

X

For the last decade or so of his life, my father and I were on good terms, and in the last couple of years became, I think, good friends. During that period I was on unpaid leave from Victoria University and over in England doing research for a biography of Kipling. I needed a job and ended up teaching at a school in Worcester for five terms. My parents, still in the same house, generously offered to have me to stay, and I gratefully accepted. A further complication in my life at the time was that my marriage was falling apart, and I was about to end it. I obviously had to break the news of this to my parents. I really had no idea how my father, in particular, would react. Would he feel ashamed of me? After all, none of his friends' children had got divorced. Would he consider it socially unacceptable? Consider it unthinkable because of the children? Fly into a rage? Try to talk me out of it? Tell me to leave the house? Any or all of these reactions seemed possible, even likely. In fact, what happened was different, showing me then and reminding me now how little I ever understood him. He heard me out in silence, and when I had finished, all he said was: 'Are you absolutely sure? Have you really thought this through?' And when I answered that I was sure and had thought it through, he said: 'All right, then we needn't discuss that side of it any more'. And we didn't, though he was enormously helpful and supportive over the complicated consequences of the separation.

XI

My father had hoped to die quickly and with dignity, and so he did. He had a heart attack in November 1992. After a couple of days on life-support in hospital, he was told that his only chance of recovery lay in a massive operation. It was characteristic of him that one of his last actions was to make sure that if he died, my mother would have immediate access to his bank account – characteristic, too, that for all the years of their marriage he had insisted on separate accounts. He never came round from the operation. He had the heart attack on Tuesday, and they switched off the life-support on Sunday.

Stroke
Tubed and wired, naked
beneath the single sheet,
my father's all there;

just a little baffled
by the casual way
they talk in the ward.

"It's Moira, Clare, Steve,
and Paul," he says. "I don't
know their proper names."

Outside it's warm, perhaps sunny.
At school Nicholas or Matt or Rich
will be giving someone else

a hard time. They're not bad kids,
just ill at ease with themselves.
Up on the fifth floor, father's worse

but hanging on. It's not what
happens to us that matters;
it's what we think has happened.

True or false? I can't decide.
Persuasion's a comfort.
This coffee tastes of burnt acorns.

Even more tubes now, more wires.
Coloured graphs scribble heart beat,
blood pressure. Numbers pulse

and change. Father's chest goes up
down, up down, up down.
His eyes flick open, shut.

His hand in mine is warm.
His feet seem to be
trussed up in silver paper.

The end when it came
was peaceful and quick.
You were there breathing

and then you weren't.
After they'd taken off
all the tubes and wires

you looked more like your
old self, but so still.
I wish we'd said goodbye.

(FROM *HOW THINGS ARE*, 1996)

THE WAY OF
DISPOSSESSION

PETER RUSSELL on *HUGH RUSSELL*

The Wound

'Then it was that the wound broke open for the first time in a long night,' Franz Kafka wrote near the end of his life to Milena Jesenská. He was referring to the night of 22–23 September 1912 when, in a trance-like state, he had given birth to the story which was to be his literary breakthrough, *The Judgement*. Surrendering to the subconscious confusion of his feelings about his father, he experienced what he called a 'complete opening of body and soul'. In forcing his hero into suicide he cleansed himself – and had before him his first masterpiece.

In writing this, I too am breaking open a wound. Should it be opened, and in public? It's a different wound from Kafka's, one already probed in long years of psychoanalysis. It should be long since healed: my father died 13 years ago at 80, and I'm now 52. It's more than 20 years since I was last in psychiatric treatment. Yet the wound has never healed. Growing into middle age has brought understanding; but *tout comprendre* has not – or not yet – resulted in *tout pardonner*. I think of my father with dismay, and without affection.

This isn't because we fell out. We never had an argument. We couldn't. In our family, feelings weren't discussed, and emotions such as anger were taboo. My father and I were always civil to each other, sensible – but strangers. There was no *relationship*. Moreover, there was no sign of awareness on his part that this was so. Nothing of significance ever passed between me and my father. I don't think he knew what it meant to have a son. And now, where my father ought to be in my mind, there's nothing. He *was* not there, and he *is* not there. *Deus absconditus.* I'm sure that my atheism since the age of 20 has much to do with the absence of a relationship with my father.

To some this must sound petulant and self-centred. I don't know how to get around that. The last thing I would want is to use this as an opportunity for self-justification, for apportioning blame. As a literary scholar, I'm acutely conscious of the limitation of a single individual's perspective. I'm equally conscious that all conclusions are provisional: that what I think at 52 is different from what I thought at 42 and what I shall think at 62. As I've grown older, too, I've become more and more aware of the infinite roots and ramifications of any individual's experience: of how much, in my case, my relationship with my father owed not only to his personality and mine, but to our ancestry, our genes, our relative ages, our siblings; the society and culture in which he, and later I, grew up; the education he and I were given; and the nature of the woman he married, and all the complexities *her* personality and background brought into the equation. I can't think of my father now, indeed, without thinking that in a different country things might have been different.

Who can ever get to the bottom of these mysteries? What's offered here is a fallible truth, subject to correction by others' truths. Indeed the comments of my wife and my three sisters have already resulted in several revisions and additions. My wife thinks my view of my father is unbalanced and suggests that the difference between his extroverted nature and my introverted one made it difficult for him to form a relationship with me. She is also exasperated at my combination of passivity and intellectualisation. While each of my three sisters sees my father differently, two see him more positively than I do. My mother would certainly have rejected my portrait of my father: she never discussed with me how I felt about him, and never wavered from the precept instilled in her by her own upbringing that absolute respect for one's father is one of the necessary pillars of the cosmos. Yet she more than anyone else ensured that I couldn't possibly respect him. I could never have written this essay while she was still living.

That I accepted an invitation to do so only weeks after her death (at 83) of course exposes me to the reproach that I'm laying charges to which the defendants have no opportunity to reply, doing this moreover from a position of privilege: with the benefit of years of psychoanalysis and with hindsight. That has certainly caused me mind-searching – exacerbated by the fact that one of my father's arsenal of Latin tags was *'De mortuis nil nisi bonum'* [Of the dead speak nothing but good]. Yet despite these misgivings I decided to write, both to clarify my own mind and in the hope that it might be of help to others to read of someone with problems which were so severe in part because they were never discussed between those who shared them, and never could be discussed.

Of course they should have been discussed. Why weren't they discussed? Initially because my psychoanalysis resulted in so complete a disparity of perspectives between me and my parents that it couldn't be bridged – or not without their sacrificing beliefs too precious to them to lose. Later, I decided consciously that it could only distress them, and serve no useful purpose, to be confronted with what I believed to be the truth. Was this a lack of courage on my part, or was it wisdom? I still incline to think the latter: I don't believe my father in particular would have been either willing or able to change the way he thought, at his advanced age (62 when I broke down). But of one thing I am sure: that in opting for restraint and silence I was behaving in the way they wanted me to behave. For it was the way we children had always been taught to behave: resisting all aggressive impulses ('If you haven't anything nice to say, say nothing'), being considerate of others, polite at all times, respectful of our elders, and always behaving in consonance with the prevailing precepts of personal and social 'normality'.

The understanding of mental illness permitted by this 'normality' was limited. Not that my parents were ignorant of the explorations of modern psychology: several Penguins in the bookshelves revealed that my mother, at least, was interested and informed. But when I began at the age of 19 to suffer from bouts of depression which became ever more severe and uncontrollable, the reaction was irrational and unhelpful. My mother, who had a friend with a history of repeated admissions to psychiatric hospital, was fearful of the social consequences ('You don't want to go to Ashburn Hall: people will look at you sideways for the rest of your life'). She insisted that I must have been over-working at university; and when I was treated with anti-depressant drugs, she became obsessed with the notion that the drugs themselves were causative.

What did my father think? I don't know, because it was always my mother who dealt with any matters relating to my personal welfare.

During the wretched process of breakdown over the summer vacation of 1965–66 when I was at home deeply depressed, I can only remember my father once getting exasperated with my unnatural taciturnity. On the day I was admitted to Ashburn Hall in April 1966, he departed on a long-planned trip around the world lasting more than three months, from which he sent letters about his travels which included the hope that I'd get better soon. Subsequently the entire matter of my mental illness was only ever mentioned by him once, that I can remember. It must have been a year or two later. We were sitting together at home – or more accurately, sitting in the same room – when he suddenly said (I'm recording this as faithfully as I can at a distance of almost 30 years): 'There's been some rumour – I've no idea at all where it came from, because it's completely wrong – that your period in Ashburn Hall has something to do with the way you were brought up. Well, I just want to make it clear that that's absolute stuff and nonsense: you were brought up with nothing but love and affection.' I can't remember how I replied to this directive, which was clearly aimed not at opening discussion but at closing it; probably I said nothing. But I do remember how my father continued: 'Love and affection,' he then mused, 'there's really no difference in meaning between those two words, is there? They mean exactly the same thing.' I can't remember how I responded to that either.

The flight from emotion into semantics was characteristic. Anything – anything at all! – rather than deal with feelings. As I'll explain later, my father had in my view grown up as an intelligent man whose intellect was well developed, but whose emotional development had never emerged from adolescence. My own breakdown, I believe, resulted from the same disparity expressed even more extremely, an imbalance which at adolescence provoked so strident a tension that my psyche began to scream. The world saw a man widely regarded as a model of sanity afflicted with a son who was going insane. But what the world sees is rarely more than a fraction of the truth.

I don't think my father could have understood that, either then or since. He was a very rational man, but it was a rationality of a limited, logical kind, not that rationality which comes of emotional integration and implies a quality of balance and sense that is embedded in feeling. While he was thus an able solicitor, and a successful husband and father in the practical sense, he was limited in personal, and especially intimate relationships. While my three sisters found him a satisfactory father, that must have been because he found his daughters easier to relate to than his son. He certainly didn't find it easy to relate to me; and at the most crucial crisis in my life he didn't relate to me at all. As a rational man, he didn't understand my depression because it was irrational: if there was no good reason for something, it was thereby invalidated. Since I'd been brought up with 'love and affection', and with every material advantage and incentive for success, there was no reason at all for me to be depressed: it was inexplicable and a nuisance. When it became clear, after a sojourn in psychiatric wards first in Timaru then in Christchurch, that I would need to go to Ashburn Hall, he (grumblingly) did the rational, the decent thing, and paid the fees. But there could be no rational grounds for postponing his long-arranged overseas trip, and as far as I can judge he enjoyed it enormously. On his return, laden with slides, both the *Southland Times* and the *Southland News* reported on his travels in three-column articles: 'City Solicitor Home after World Tour'.

A different son, emerging from such an ordeal, might have sought confrontation. I didn't: I battled my problems alone, and remained what I'd always been, a 'good' boy, preserving good relations with my parents as a result. Of course it meant coolness; but that had been the norm anyway. As mentioned, apart from that one sally, the matter of my illness was never again mentioned by my father, and indeed nothing remotely personal passed between us until his death. My mother also never showed signs of wanting to discuss the matter, although she did, curiously, on our family's last summer visit to her when she was 82, let slip a comment which suggests that, given a few more years, she and I might have come to some kind of understanding. In response to what must have been a critical remark I made about my father, she said hastily that she could see now that things couldn't have been easy for me as a boy . . . But she didn't explain what she meant, and clearly found the subject difficult. Nothing more was said. A few months later she suffered a severe stroke, and she died soon afterwards.

I don't remember anyone suggesting I speak at my father's funeral in 1984, and I couldn't have done so. His death was followed by an ordeal of six months in which I wrestled with feelings of anger and worthlessness. But when, in 1996, my sisters asked me to provide a funeral eulogy for my mother, I had little difficulty in putting together a genial, positive and, I think, reasonably just portrait of her, as I knew her family and friends liked to see her. Much laughter was provoked by my comments on my mother's doting attitude to children and what she believed essential for their upbringing; few will have sensed their deadly serious undertones. Only when it came to the necessity of saying something laudatory about my father, and my mother's 42-year marriage to him, did I have difficulty. I resorted of necessity to commonplace pieties, for I was speaking before a large congregation of people who were friends and admirers of my mother. Many of them had been friends and admirers of my father, too. My father had numerous admirers: they certainly weren't wrong in this. It's just that they weren't his son.

The Family

My father was the third in a line of Irish lawyers in Invercargill, in an unbroken tradition of legal practice there which had been begun in 1862 by my great-grandfather William and continued by my grandfather Eustace.

William was the youngest son of Thomas Russell senior, who had in 1840 arrived in northern New Zealand from Cork. Thomas Russell had a large family which was to spawn no fewer than four separate New Zealand law firms, each surviving today, albeit in altered form. William married in 1862, and in the same year he and his wife left Auckland by ship for Invercargill; there he opened a law practice and in 1871 became the first district land registrar, as well as farming a small property on the Bay Road just to the north of what was then but a village at the edge of the bush. They had six children.

His son Eustace, who was admitted to the bar in 1898, practised law in Invercargill for 45 years. Throughout his life a sportsman of prowess, he was a man of fierce physical and mental energies, which went into establishing both the Invercargill Golf Club and a reputation as the city's leading criminal lawyer. He was also famous for his talkativeness. He married in 1902 and, in the same year, built the imposing home in spacious grounds in Herbert Street, north Invercargill, where my father and his two sisters were brought up. After being sent to preparatory school at Waihi in South Canterbury, then to Christ's College in Christchurch, and studying law at Otago University, my father then lived out his life until retirement at 71 in Invercargill within the circumference of a few hundred metres. He didn't go to the Second World War; none of

HUGH RUSSELL AT 22

us knows why or apparently ever asked. He lived at home until he married; upon marrying he moved with his bride into a house built by his twin sister and her husband – a two-minute walk round the corner in Lewis Street; a few years later, he built a home of his own on what had been the orchard of his parents' house, inheriting their vegetable garden and tennis court. In a certain sense he never left home.

My father married late, at 38; my mother was nine-and-a-half years his junior. A woman friend of his once told me he was long regarded as Invercargill's most eligible bachelor, but had been given up as a lost cause. The fact that he married so late, and was therefore older than most fathers are when his four children were born (39–46), combined with the fact that he was an only son who had lived so long at home under the devoted care of his mother, certainly had an influence on the nature of his relationship with his own only son. Not to mention his relationship with his wife: I remember my mother saying how he upset her after they married by going to visit his mother every evening! Shortly after marriage, my father contracted meningitis and lost all hearing; following treatment he emerged with no hearing in one ear and impaired hearing in the other. My elder sister has pointed out that his deafness had an isolating effect on him in the family: he would, for example, often sit reading with little awareness of the conversation around him. His deafness must certainly have contributed to his self-absorbed air.

My father inherited the energy and impatience of his own father, and both came from a race of garrulous, clever, sceptical Irish lawyers. My mother came from the very different background of an impoverished Anglican vicarage of exemplary piety. Unlike most migrants from the Old World – the people who, like Thomas Russell senior, came to New Zealand to seek their fortune – my mother's father, John Lush, emigrated in obedience to Christian ideals.

John Lush's devotion to God and the Church was wholehearted. Though they were themselves desperately hard up, money went to the parish poor, not to his daughters. Not only that, but when St John's Girls' preparatory school got into financial difficulties in the Depression, he rescued it by putting his daughters to teach there without salary. My mother, who had attended St Margaret's College in Christchurch on a scholarship for the daughters of clergy, and had left with an outstanding academic, sporting and musical record (a brilliant pianist, she did her LTCL while still at school), was stopped in mid-career. This she fiercely resented; all her life the privations of her childhood, and her father's treatment of her, were to be obsessive themes. There was much anger in her which never found an outlet: how could it, given the fixed Christian obedience in which she and her two sisters were raised? Yet when challenged on the point by me, my mother insisted indignantly that she never regarded her father with anything but complete love and respect – like everyone else. This fierce, unadmitted ambivalence had, I believe, profound consequences both for her marriage and for my own upbringing. For in her relationship with her husband was repeated, and sustained for 42 years, the same unadmitted ambivalence of anger and love. It would be transmitted to me in the form of the constant, destructive belittlement of my father.

She and my father had met at tennis at his parents' court; they became engaged and married at the end of 1941. Without wishing to seem cynical, I'm certain that one of the attractions my father held for her was wealth. My elder sister was born in 1942, myself in 1945, and two more sisters in 1948 and 1950. I remember my mother relating that on her return to New Zealand from the two years she spent in Europe, she went through a period of depression and great emotional confusion (a pattern later to be repeated in her son), but that once she had 'a quiver full of little kiddies' she was just fine. I've never forgotten that extraordinary metaphor: both because it suggests that it wasn't marriage that cured her of her woes, but the procreation of children; and also because she seems to have regarded us children as arrows. Arrows for what? I presume as missiles to shoot at her depression.

Early Childhood

My mother loved mothering and was a very child-centred person. She was a resourceful, outgoing, hugely generous person, and despite the spectacular evidence to the contrary, held all her life to two unshakable beliefs: that children could do no wrong, and that all they needed was love. Needless to say, children also loved her for this reason. In her enthusiastic dedication to the role of mother she was of her time: in those years of stability and conformity after the turmoil of war, the chief desire of most women was the opportunity to bring up a family in peace and quiet and the role of mothers in particular has probably never received such general social and political support. It was also a generation which required of men only a limited participation in their children's upbringing. In a practical sense my father conscientiously fulfilled the duties expected of a father at the time, and in that sense he was a good father, devoted and responsible. He provided for our material welfare, used to take us for drives or for visits to the museum on Sunday mornings, and read to us in bed. If I were asked to describe happy times spent with my father, it would be those evenings when he read to me as a child in bed, or himself made up stories for me, something he was good at. I think they were happy times for him too, in part because they enabled him to relive his own childhood. Certainly many of the books he read to me were ones he'd had himself as a boy, both British children's classics (Richard Jefferies' *Bevis* remains a pleasant memory) and boys' adventure fiction of the period. Because of my father's age, a curiosity of my childhood was that, in the 1950s, he brought me up on tales of doughty British boyhood in the Empire as it existed before and during the First World War! The excitement of Submarine U93 still lives in my imagination.

However, the attachment to his own childhood which my father showed in this activity was, I believe, also symptomatic of something deeper: an arrested emotional growth. Years of psychoanalysis and reflection have led me to believe that my mother must have learnt fairly soon that the man she had married, while being an affectionate spouse, a civilised companion and a successful lawyer who would provide her and their children with a comfortable life, was emotionally childlike. I'm sure that neither the realisation itself, nor the ways in which she sought to adjust to the situation she found herself in, was conscious: I'm speaking here of those ceaseless subtle shifts and adaptations that keep occurring in any close relationship. But the shifts which occurred were, I believe, in three respects to have a warping influence on my upbringing.

First, I believe that my mother, finding my father emotionally frustrating, early on unconsciously displaced on to her children, and in particular on to her only son, the love that would usually have been satisfied by a husband, seeking in mothering the emotional satisfactions she couldn't find in being a wife. Second, having been convinced by her own experience that authoritarian fathers were a villainous source of human misery, she made sure her own husband would be nothing of the sort, assuming herself all the essential rearing functions, including disciplining us. My father had no role to play in my emotional development, unless prompted to do so by my mother. (I remember, for example, that on the eve of my departure for boarding school he admonished me to shun boys who indulged in sexual misbehaviour: what was so awful about this was not so much his understandable nervous embarrassment, but that he had so obviously been told by my mother to see to this.) Third, in my adolescence and afterwards, when it became crucial that I had a strong male figure whom I could look up to, my mother incessantly kept impressing on her son that his father was in reality no more than a child. Indeed, when I broke down at 20, the explanation she gave me as to why there was no question of his postponing his world trip was that he was 'as excited as a child' about it. This belittlement of my father continued for years after my breakdown: letters she wrote to me after my marriage, during our years overseas from 1968 to 1972, regularly conveyed this perception of him. (My elder sister has told me how sorry she too felt for our father at times, when our mother criticised or spoke ill of him to others.) In one sense my mother can't be blamed for this: she was describing a reality which clearly caused her continuing frustration, probably more and more so as my father aged. But her attitude only made things worse for her son, a son who had broken down once, and was to break down again.

Outwardly, my parents' marriage was highly successful, certainly in a social sense. I don't think it involved passion, or not for long. But they got on well together, seldom quarrelled (my two younger sisters remember their quarrels better than I do), and ran their marriage as a kind of efficient business partnership, based on an agreed division of labour and the conscientious fulfilment of duties: it was a way satisfactory to them both of making the marriage work. It was a physically undemonstrative partnership, and indeed both my parents were physically undemonstrative people.

The only physical contact I ever had with my father was to shake his hand when I departed for or returned from boarding school: as he did so, he never looked at me, but sideways down at the ground. While my mother presumably hugged us as children, I can't remember it, and certainly after the age of 12 I never experienced an embrace: until her death at 83, the most I ever knew was the exchange of a hasty, nervous peck on the cheek. But in a more general sense neither of them invited shared intimacy, from me or from anyone else. While my mother was a warm, outgoing person, she was also a powerful personality who, by always making the other person the focus of her full attention, at the same time made herself emotionally unassailable.

But socially, they were an unbeatable pair. They were both immensely sociable and hospitable people, and visitors were constant. The house was well stocked with books and magazines, constantly being lent or exchanged. There was also much singing around the piano. Neighbours and friends came for bridge or tennis; my mother held women's tennis parties during the week, and there was regular men's tennis (most players being local lawyers) on Saturday afternoons. Owing to Invercargill's climate, this usually meant getting out after lunch with buckets and mops. At afternoon tea, the men would sit together in their whites in the sun porch and talk men's talk: whether they'd got their lettuces planted yet, how their shares were doing, the merits of the latest models of car, New Zealand's fortunes at cricket, rugby, or Wimbledon. Thus I learnt what it meant to be a man. On the afternoon of Christmas Day, crowds came – for tennis, Christmas cake, mini-golf on the front lawn, and a sing-song round the piano.

As all this implies, my parents were both resolute extroverts, and in my father's case this took an extreme form. In the term used by Doctor Johnson to describe Boswell (of whom my father was a fan), he was 'a very clubable man', and indeed was a member and regular patron of the Invercargill Club from the age of 32 until his retirement and move to Arrowtown at 71. A short, wiry man, with a lively intellect and an inexhaustible fund of anecdotes, jokes and conundrums, he liked nothing better than the opportunity to tell them; he was also a dab hand at doggerel verse. In retrospect, I wonder if he had an inner life at all. I remember a friend of his telling him that he was so well-read and entertaining a person that he should write his memoirs; my father just shook his head. He was right: he couldn't have written his memoirs, because he didn't reflect upon himself, and defined himself day by day by the society he was in. Yet he was also one of the most self-absorbed people I ever knew, with the innocent, oblivious self-absorption typical of a child. His phenomenal energy into old age reflected this; phenomenally energetic men are often boylike. My father's perpetually boyish quality appealed to many, especially maternal women. But it was of no use to his son.

In a material sense, we had a comfortable and privileged life. Not only did New Zealand at the time lead the world in its standard of living, but my father was fond of pointing out that Southland had the highest per capita income in New Zealand. He always voted National. He benefited from inheritance: not only from his parents, who died in 1953 and 1954, but also from the wealthy Thomas Russell of the previous generation, who had in his will bestowed unusual largesse on his brothers. From 1951, we lived in a large, new, two-storeyed house with all mod cons. A gardener, inherited from my grandparents, came on Saturday morning; a cleaning woman, also inherited, came several mornings a week. As a child I never had to make my own bed. I can see now that in intensely conservative Invercargill I absorbed as a child a kind of class consciousness, an awareness of master-servant relationships, which had characterised pre-war Britain. This would also serve me well at Christ's College, whose headmaster once earnestly exhorted his charges in a prize-giving speech to take to heart the meaning of *noblesse oblige*. I well remember the outrage of a Marxist friend when I related the fact some years later; similarly vivid is my wife's anger at my mother's seigneurial manner of referring to the cleaning woman by her surname only. She also used to refer slightingly to the 'Bog Irish' of south Invercargill, who she said had merely been brought in as migrant workers to build the railway, but had settled! Although the same Irish of south Invercargill made up a good proportion of my father's clients and thus presumably contributed to our high standard of living, they earned his displeasure as well by being Roman Catholic: he regarded this faith all his life as a risible affront to reason. But my parents were decent employers, and themselves both hard-working people. They worked hard at their pleasures, too. In 1950, when I was five, they had a holiday house built at Arrowtown in Central Otago, where we spent our school holidays and frequent weekends as well. In summer we picnicked, swam, boated, water-skied and fought each other up and down the table-tennis ladder; in winter we skied at Coronet Peak, skated at the Arrowtown ice-rink and played board-games in front of a roaring pine fire. There was fun, companionship, and much laughter.

I was apparently always a good boy, 'easy'. My childhood was normal in every external sense: I went to school, played a lot of tennis with friends, built huts with them, devoured Richmal Crompton's 'William' books and Enid Blyton's 'Famous Five', collected stamps, busied myself with carpentry, and biked to the Tepid Baths, the cinema, and to Saturday morning sessions at the YMCA. In summer we tirelessly played a vigorous game called 'Kick the Tin' in the garden with friends; or we braved the breakers of vast Oreti Beach, skidded down the sand-dunes, spied on lovers and ate hot-dogs. The doors of the house never had to be locked during the day, except when we went to Arrowtown – and even then the back door was left propped open for the family cat to go in and out. There were holidays too on the farm of my mother's sister and her husband at Centre Bush, with lamb-feeding, horse-riding and swimming in the willow-fringed Oreti River. My elder sister kept her own horse near Invercargill, and the three girls all went to ballet lessons and learnt the piano, while I learnt the violin. Apart from the Royal Tour of 1954, Invercargill offered few excitements, except as provided by the sound of fire engines: my friends and I always jumped on our bikes and pedalled madly in pursuit. As my father was an avid photographer, and for a time had his own dark-room, our childhood is exhaustively documented: I appear as a happy if perhaps over-thoughtful child. 'Peter is a thinker', my mother was prone to say. I was certainly a bookworm, and also spent long solitary hours in my bedroom with stamp collection or crystal set; according to one of my sisters, my mother was constantly trying to lure me out. From the age of seven, I began to write much poetry which, like everything else I did, was greeted with uncritical adulation by my mother and fostered her lifelong conviction that I was a genius destined for celebrity. Possessed of a good treble voice, I also sang in the local church choir and was enthusiastically religious, attending church at all three Sunday services.

Education

Such habits of piety served me well when, at 12, I left home in an uncomfortable grey suit, my first long trousers, a starched Peter Pan collar and a black-and-white tie, to become a boarder at Christ's College in Christchurch, like my father before me. I'd been enrolled at birth. Needless to say, geographical distance (555 kilometres, a whole day's journey by steam train) intensified the emotional distance already existing between me and my father.

Christ's College, New Zealand's oldest private school, had been founded in 1850 as a colonial replica of the English public school, and a century later this ideal was still being grafted onto a population of boys who, in the boarding-houses at least, were mainly the robustly indifferent offspring of farmers with enough money to pay the fees. Initially, I was frightened and desperately homesick. Within my first month I was twice caned: for 'moving cutlery before grace' and for 'talking before grace'; neither (to my knowledge) had infringed rules. The canings, conducted with portentous ceremony by the house prefects after evening prayers, were a terrifying experience: I made sure I never broke any rule again in my five years at school.

But I found myself in an environment which taught and enforced stoicism: I learnt it. Anxiety, vulnerability, unhappiness: all were repressed. I worked hard, did my best to keep out of trouble, and conscientiously applied myself to doing what the school demanded of me, which included a year of playing cricket, which I disliked (I then switched to tennis); and five years of playing rugby, which I hated. As always I was a 'good' boy, and very religious: prayer became an essential prop to my existence. On Sundays after chapel, the only time we were allowed out, I mostly used to visit two maiden great-aunts (sisters of my father's mother), mow their lawns and read books.

While early on I had intense friendships with two much older boys, I largely remained a loner among boys of my own age; no friendships survived beyond school. This was in part because I was isolated by my enthusiasms, which didn't include the manly physical pursuits extolled by the school (and bizarrely equated by it with something called 'leadership'), but were focused on such effete pastimes as playing in the school orchestra, singing in the madrigal group and performing as treble soloist in the chapel choir. Increasingly, too, I became absorbed by the reading of literature, which from the sixth form included French literature.

My insecurity was no doubt exacerbated by the fact that both physically and intellectually I matured unusually late. At 15 I was head treble; at fifteen-and-a-half my mother had a record made of my treble singing; and when in the sixth form my voice proved as treble as ever, the music master shifted me into the altos to spare me embarrassment! During that year a long-delayed growth spurt brought a sudden intellectual blossoming – with the result that in my final year, as unexpectedly for myself as for others, I streaked ahead academically, won a very large number of prizes, and was named dux. (I later learnt from my mother that my excited father had got hold of as many copies of the prize list as he could and posted them off to relatives.) I then went with scholarships to Canterbury University, boarding for three years at Christchurch College, an Anglican theological college and student hostel, and continued my academic success, receiving an A pass in all my BA courses, as well as fitting in three law courses before deciding during my second year to throw in law. Although the family law practice had by now celebrated its centenary and I was the sole male successor (my five cousins on the Russell side were all girls, and girls didn't study law), no pressure was put on me to step into my father's shoes.

Then came my increasingly unstable third year, violent mood-swings, ever more savage depression, and breakdown. I was much helped during the year by the kind and understanding doctor at the university's medical service, without whose support I couldn't have got through the examinations. My letters home must have given alarm signals, for I remember that my father at this time wrote me a letter – I'm sure at my mother's instigation – suggesting that I was too devoted to study and should set about enjoying myself more. Seldom could a letter have been more beside the point. In any case, no mere external agency, and least of all my father, could now rescue the rudderless ship from the currents bearing it into the storm.

Did I have a happy childhood? It's a question I can't answer. It was idyll and trauma at once: outwardly privileged, ordered and very sheltered, but inwardly confused and problematic. Before my breakdown I would have said: yes, my childhood was happy. But since then I've been so aware of the forces gathering during that childhood which were to culminate in prolonged anguish that I have to answer: no. I certainly have many specific happy memories. But emotionally my childhood was a disaster; because it didn't prepare me for adulthood.

At 17, after a fallow period during adolescence, I suddenly began writing poetry again, one of whose chief themes is the panic and bewilderment of losing childhood: it stammers the distress of a boy who doesn't know how to become a man, whose gaze is fixed back but who, finding no way of going forward, is condemned to maddened introspection. My literary idols were Dylan Thomas and Oscar Wilde: an unlikely pairing, but perhaps what unites them is precisely that both turned arrested emotional development to brilliant literary use. But I hadn't their genius. When some of my poetry appeared in the school magazine, my mother expressed astonishment that so apparently happy a boy should write such morbid poetry. She was right to wonder: the puzzle would be clarified three years later. I can't remember my father making any comment. He wouldn't have liked my poetry; his own tastes had been for Kipling and the Georgians, and in any case in him poetry reading had long since yielded to a diet of thrillers, and *Punch* and *Time* magazines.

Because I've drawn so negative a portrait of my father, I'd like to end this section by redressing the balance somewhat. There's no reason why a man's son should be his best judge, and those seeing him from other perspectives must have a more positive view of him. My father was a good man, a man of integrity and without malice. His friends found in him a determined opponent at squash, tennis, golf, snooker, and bridge, and a hospitable, sociable, mentally agile and always entertaining companion. His clients, I'm sure, found him an efficient, scrupulously honest, kindly solicitor and adviser. Many would have reason to speak of his generosity – particularly those impecunious clients to whom he gave services free of charge. Children loved him for his conjuring tricks. And late in life he did his bit for the community, chairing the Marriage Guidance Council and the library committee and sitting on the Plunket Advisory Board. After retirement to Arrowtown at 71, he worked for the establishment of a public library there, and continued energetic and active to the end: the stroke which hospitalised him for his last two years came on a day when, at 78, he had followed a round of golf by a set of tennis. His obituary in the *Southland Times*, while shorter than his father's and grandfather's before him, depicts a successful man. He was also grateful for his life, which had been remarkably free of difficulty. His last preserved letter, penned from hospital in Invercargill to his wife in Arrowtown, was written shakily with the left hand because the stroke had disabled his right side, but its message is unambiguous: 'To Dear Mother with love with thanks for all you did for me. Best love Hugh.'

Breakdown

This section can be brief, for I've already said much about my breakdown and my parents' role in it. It would be unbalanced and unfair to claim they were (singly or jointly) the sole factor precipitating my breakdown, for a whole variety of influences contributed to the difficulties I experienced in growing from boyhood to manhood. As for the deepening neurosis itself and its more pathological manifestations: this is not the place to go into those details, and it would embarrass me to do so.

But two general aspects of my illness could be recorded here from the vantage-point of hindsight. First, the more depressed and isolated I became, the more fanatically obsessed I grew with my ambition of becoming a writer and nothing but a writer: this became for me the only possible answer to my maladjustment to society and the only acceptable explanation of my unstable condition. Reading Nietzsche and Rilke had moreover convinced me that there was no god and that in art lay the only possible metaphysical activity of mankind.

Second, the initial revelations of my psychoanalytic treatment caused me to experience my problem in terms of an overpowering mother; and I'm sure my (Freudian) analyst likewise believed he'd raised the lid on yet another perfect specimen of the Oedipus Complex. However, with increasing age I came to attribute less and less importance to my mother's role in my becoming ill, and more and more to my father's. My mother, I think, was always the more mature person, and that became evident in the following years, when my hostility to her yielded to restored affection. This didn't happen with my father, who in old age seamlessly slipped into Shakespeare's 'second childishness' without having emerged from his first – and without ever giving the slightest hint of being aware what his son thought of him.

The Legacy

Needless to say, I owe a great many positive things to my parents: through my genes I've inherited qualities of mind and character, and through my upbringing attitudes and habits of behaviour, which have served me in good stead throughout my life. Of qualities inherited from my father, the one I most value is his sense of humour. My wife and children think I've inherited his impatience, and my sisters would add intolerance, and inflexibility about meal-times. I wish I had his energy. I've also benefited materially, not only in the sense that I grew up in a cultivated home and was provided with a good education, but also because of my parents' continuing financial generosity to their children and grandchildren, which has been a boon to us all. In the following, however, I'll focus on what I think may have been some specific results of my problematic lack of relationship with my father, and my experience of mental illness.

The immediate effect of my illness was a despair which was frequently suicidal. I endured what remains the worst suffering of my life. It was worst of all when, at Ashburn Hall, I was withdrawn over three months from all medication and began a psychoanalysis. The panic-stricken resistances with which a defensive personality reacts to the first probes of therapy mean that depression worsens before it starts getting better. I feel now for psychiatrists who have to guide their patients through that first stage when suicide is so real a danger. It was then a process of moving, over years, from one fiercely resisted insight to the next: altogether a long, slow and excruciating haul. After I was pushed out of hospital in March 1967 to do my honours degree, treatment had to continue: regular interviews with a psychiatrist twice a week for a further year, then once a week until I married in July 1968 and my wife and I left New Zealand. Even that wasn't the end: on our return to New Zealand four years later, I again succumbed to depression and had to undergo further lengthy treatment. I regard it as my great good fortune to have been a patient at that time of the skilled and wise John Hardwick-Smith.

It's a cliché, but also a profound truth, that suffering has its own purpose, that in retrospect our worst experiences may prove to have been our best, and even that concealed in apparently dead-end despair is what later proves to have been of most value for our lives. It's an

PETER RUSSELL AT 22

insight found in myth and religion, and given memorable expression in Western literature by Virgil, Dante, Goethe, Nietzsche, and Rilke. While the latter two obsessively haunted the prison of my illness, closer to my heart today is the quiet formulation of T. S. Eliot in *Four Quartets*, where he describes coming into possession 'by the way of dispossession'. This is a good way of describing in retrospect my experience of mental illness. To my forced hospitalisation in Ashburn Hall, which my mother had prophesied would stigmatise me for life, I on the contrary directly owe the best things in my adult life: my marriage and my career. First and most important, it was there that I met and fell in love with the exceptional woman, then aged 18, to whom I have had the good fortune to be married for 29 years and who has borne our four children. My parents' anxiety must have been extreme when they learnt that I wished to marry a fellow patient, but she won them over at once and was taken to their hearts, for which I've always been most grateful. Second, through the necessity for continued psychiatric treatment which forced me to exchange Canterbury University for Otago, I unexpectedly found myself studying with a professor to whose international repute and vigorous support I was to owe the first vital appointments in my academic career (in Germany, then Britain); at Canterbury neither that repute nor that support would have been my lot. I also made good friends at the university who are still friends today.

The lesson that possession comes by the way of dispossession was painfully learnt again by us both when our first two children, a son and then a year later a daughter, both died of an illness which baffled medical science. Understandably, it was a more terrible experience for their mother than for their father. But it confirmed all my worst fears about myself: I, who had struggled so long, and against such doubt, to become a man, had tried to become a father and had failed. In the end it was a growing experience that strengthened our marriage. Our two following children, now in their teens, seem determined to compensate in robustness and rude health for the helpless illness of their predecessors. (They also delight in making rude remarks about the 'loony bin' background of their parents.) Like hospitalisation in Ashburn Hall, our bereavement also had an unforeseeable positive professional outcome: it led me to a detailed study of Mahler's *Songs on the Death of Children*, to a PhD thesis, a book, fruitful contact with a leading Mahler authority, and promotion to associate professor.

If I look for the longer-term legacy of my deficient relationship with my father, numerous thoughts come to mind. One effect was certainly a prolonged search for a substitute father-figure: a doomed quest, because none of those I fixed on were interested in playing this role in my life. They were usually professors under whom I was either studying or in employment. This is, of course, a natural process in a young man's life, perhaps particularly so at universities: not for nothing do Germans call the supervisor of a PhD thesis the *'Doktorvater'*. But in me, as I only later realised, the need was unnatural and unnaturally prolonged; it brought repeated frustration and sadness.

A deeper effect on my life has been, as I hinted earlier, a dogged atheism, with the accompanying conviction that human life is inherently meaningless and, as Doctor Johnson describes it in *Rasselas*, 'a state in which much is to be endured, and little to be enjoyed'. My experience of mental illness has also taught me the sobering lesson that there are no limits to the extent to which even highly intelligent people will blind themselves to whatever their mental household can't accommodate, or imperils their equilibrium. This I believe applied equally to me as a patient in psychoanalysis, and to my parents' response to my illness. As T. S. Eliot rightly puts it, 'human kind /Cannot bear very much reality'. Related is my conviction that the price of human happiness is vigilant self-scrutiny. The unexamined life of my father exacted as its price the over-examined life of his son. The surfaces of normality are deceptive: the ordinary and familiar conceal warps which may foster madness. There is a narrow line of sanity in life, and on either side of it horror. Sanity has to be worked at. My long fascination with German culture, and especially the phenomenon of Nazism, is associated with this.

I began by referring to Kafka's *The Judgement*, and by wondering if I, like he, should break open a personal wound in public. Readers will have made their own judgement as to whether I took the right decision. For its writer the task, while arduous, has certainly meant a gaining of clarity. Perhaps it may even prove to have been a step towards that hoped-for time in old age when, in the words of the ageing Yeats, the 'intellect grows sure / That all's arranged in one clear view'. If, as I suspect, the 'one clear view' eludes us mortals to the last, I'll hope to be granted in age at least the satisfaction of being allowed to feel that I've been a tolerable husband to my wife, and a father who hasn't bequeathed too much darkness to his children.

PORTRAIT IN SEARCH OF MY FATHER

BILL SEWELL on *ARTHUR SEWELL*

I

It was Mr Batchelor who first made me realise that teachers are human beings after all. I must have been nine or 10, and he was teaching – or trying to teach – history, the sort of history which was in no way analytical but still provides the basis of a good British general knowledge: the Domesday Book, 1086; the Long Parliament, 1640; Repeal of the Corn Laws, 1846. I don't remember why our small class of privileged boys of the 1960s was misbehaving – perhaps one of us had just given a particularly cretinous answer to a simple question – but as he was wearily trying to restore order, I felt a sudden wave of compassion for Mr Batchelor. He was a young man, probably not long out of school himself. Was this to be the sum of the rest of his life? Wouldn't he, like us, rather be somewhere else? On the sports field, in a pub, in somebody's arms? Did it really matter that the Synod of Whitby took place in AD 664?

The moment passed, of course. Small boys are too busy growing to allow compassion to occur to them as more than a possibility. The next day Mr Batchelor was the person in authority again, someone who knew the answers and who closed the door of the staff room behind him. He was not one of the outstanding teachers of my education, and I recall him only because of a novel emotion he triggered in me which had nothing to do with the quality of his teaching or what he was teaching.

Many teachers get by. They struggle through the syllabus and barely

BILL WITH
ARTHUR SEWELL

keep control. Some are simply bad: those who are incurious or ignorant, or who are unable to communicate at all with children and adolescents, or who operate through fear. In Mr Elliott's case, it was a mixture of fear and sheer evil. Mr Elliott taught mathematics. He managed to thoroughly confuse me in algebra and then had me caned for insolence. Mr Elliott is reputed to have thrown a blackboard compass at one of the senior boys; and he used to dandle one of my classmates on his knees. Mr Elliott smoked Russian cigarettes and was seen dancing one day with the matron's daughter in the staff room. Mr Elliott disappeared from the school overnight in mysterious circumstances; we were never told why but some boys (of course) claimed to be privy to the reason.

I don't want to flatter bad teachers by bringing them to mind. Better to celebrate the good teachers. Mr Milroy, for instance, a gentle man, who was probably the first to give me an inkling of what good writing is all about, the only teacher at that school in the Tory heartland to acknowledge his support for Harold Wilson and the Labour Party in the general election of 1963. Or R.O.N. ('Ronnie') Adams, my first German teacher, who managed to steer me through the stern inflections of German to an appreciation of the wonderful dynamics of that language. Finally, there was Mr Hornsby, headmaster and a much feared teacher of Latin. 'You great, great donkey!' he would shout as he flung an exercise book at some unfortunate who had still not grasped the ablative absolute. It was he who recognised that another year at school would do me no good, encouraging me to win the scholarship that took me to university at the age of 17. He also installed in me the habit of taking an interest in current affairs and started me on an early reading binge of the great Russian novelists.

As I think back, I am conscious of the lasting impact which these men, with all their prejudices and weaknesses, made on me. I am also aware that this is a response which will die with me. That is the problem with being a teacher: the effects are so ephemeral. The generations roll on, and suddenly there are no more pupils in whose memory a teacher can survive. It is largely this ephemerality which makes me want to write about my father, a teacher who never taught me as such, and my relationship with him. He was a professor of English who, as he himself said, did his 'best work' at Auckland University over half a century ago, and who has been dead for a quarter of a century.

I feel somewhat diffident at writing about Arthur because he had a deep mistrust of biography and biographers. He had a number of celebrated literary friends with whom he spent many intimate and happy hours, and with whom he corresponded from time to time. They included the poets Louis MacNeice and Rex Fairburn. But he had no intention of sharing that intimacy with third parties, least of all literary biographers. As he put it in his unfinished memoir:

> There will be lives of [the] poets who were my friends. I don't doubt it. Volumes of their letters to be pecked and cawed over. The scavengers, the vultures, littérateur leeches, literary lizards, circle and creep and dart over clay and dust. And crawl in and out of wastepaper baskets.

So contemptuous was he of literary biographers – and this was before the days of literary biography becoming such an industry – that he systematically destroyed personal papers at regular intervals throughout his life. The only material he kept back was his lectures, essays, and articles. Any personal material was preserved by chance. It makes a reconstruction of his life very difficult, all the more so since nearly all of his contemporaries either preceded or have since joined him in death.

It is not as if he was a specially private person. That could never be said of anyone who scratched his balls at the front window in full view of the neighbourhood, or who wept openly at bad movies or at the premature death of Hugh Gaitskill in 1963. What was the source of his antipathy to literary biography? I can trace it partly to a consistently held scepticism about the value of literary psychoanalysis, evident for example in his book of essays on Shakespeare, *Character and Society in Shakespeare* (1951), in which he maintained that Shakespeare's characters derive their life from 'a complex of social attitudes', and not from 'depth psychology'. And we know that bad or facile literary biography often follows the misleading road of the latter. But perhaps the antipathy also had something to do with a cussed, mischievous, even self-destructive streak of his, and a desire to thwart those who live vicariously.

Unlike Arthur, I *am* a private person: I don't want other people to know more about me than I believe is necessary. I am secretive, abhorring the thought, for instance, that somebody might peek at a draft of something I have written before it is ready for release. I like to keep my voice down in conversation, because I don't want others to eavesdrop, whatever the topic. Even so, I am an avid reader of literary biography.

But simple personal predilection in the face of Arthur's disapproval will not do. I must find some further justification for defying his wishes, and I find it in the need to capture the essence of the man. An understanding of his life, even his professional life, would be unthinkable without intruding on the personal. Because, much as he doubted the value of depth psychology in literary criticism, he was not reluctant to bring his own emotions into his teaching. And the best way I can reach them is through my own fitful and fading memory and the few personal documents he left behind. Beyond that is the larger need to try and scoop up something from the bottom of the rapidly draining basin which is his living reputation.

As I write this, I am aware of Arthur's photograph hanging to my left on the study wall, a characteristic profile portrait which shows him absorbed in reading, and I am relieved that we cannot make eye contact. It is as if we can work quietly together on our separate tasks, and I don't have to face his disappointment. A disappointment, first, at my decision to breach, however gently, the biographical barrier. And then there is another kind of disappointment, which perhaps I transfer to him: the disappointment at how I have turned out. As I have crept into middle age, I am told that I increasingly resemble Arthur – in voice, in looks, in manner – and at times, when I catch a glimpse of this behind my reflection in the mirror, I have to agree. But there are so many other respects in which I do not resemble him: in his articulateness, his wit, his intellect, his sheer brilliance, his eminence in his profession – even the fact that he *had* a profession – and most of all, in his warmth. That is a harder disappointment to have to face.

II

I only ever saw Arthur teach twice, both times during my final year at school when he was the guest speaker at meetings of an English association which involved senior school pupils. On the second occasion, I had to introduce him and, in my embarrassment, merely muttered something quickly to the audience before handing over, much to his amusement. I barely recall the lectures themselves, which may be explained by the fact that he was very frail at that stage of his life, and I was nervous at the possibility of some sort of breakdown. (As Michael King, one of his students, later wrote, Arthur 'boiled away in a body that did not seem sufficiently robust to contain his spirit'.) Two details I do remember clearly, however. Both illustrate his flair for being provocative. The first was his revelation that even Shakespeare could write sloppily at times, a prime example being the words 'And by opposing end *them*' (from Hamlet's 'To be, or not to be' soliloquy), which have an uncertain antecedent. The second related to John Donne's notion of eternity in a moment. Arthur's view was that this was a very sensible way of conceptualising eternity, because an everlasting eternity, particularly a Christian one, would be unbearably tedious. Another general memory I have is that however frail he was, and however humble the audience, he always approached the lectures as performances – so much so that throughout his life, he was physically ill before certain lectures, as if they required that special adrenalin edge familiar to many actors.

I should defer now to some of his former students, who were not inconvenienced by being his adolescent son. Here is Alan Horsman – the student of his whom he perhaps most respected as a scholar, who was to become professor of English at Otago for many years – on Arthur's early morning lectures:

> . . . *fresh from the bath, edgy, a little startled to find himself there, he gave even more than usually the impression of assessing with tingling sensibility the quality of his author. If he was introducing you to one with whom you were making a first acquaintance, it was electrifying; perhaps less so if you had some prior knowledge, but enchanting all the same from the impression that he was experiencing something of the poem or the play (he was less good on fiction) as he spoke. The actor in him controlled the timing of phrase and pause, the hesitations while apparently searching for*

*the right word ('the, the, the . . .'), or the rising intonation, sometimes with
just a trace of mockery ('Spenser (in the sonnets) is just a little heavy with
moral responsibility') but these never seemed mere tricks, but requirements
for exposition at his level of sensibility . . .*

And here is the poet Lauris Edmond, whom Arthur taught at Waikato
University, on his impact on senior school students (like myself) during
his last years:

*He would come slowly through the door of some classroom, a small slight
figure, frail, gentle in manner, white hair flowing, blue eyes deep and
penetrating. There was spontaneous attention. He achieved an immediacy
of contact by combining two contradictory styles: he could be intimate, even
confidential, while at the same time preserving the hauteur of a dignified
and fastidious scholar. He had, and used, the skills of an accomplished
actor – varied pitch and tone of voice, long pauses, a quick sensitivity to
the atmosphere of the moment. His hands he used as a kind of signal as
he spoke – No, you haven't got the point yet, he seemed to say, wait, wait
. . . here it comes . . . now, you see, it was worth waiting for, wasn't it?*

'Sensibility', 'sensitivity': what is common to these impressions is his
ability to bring feeling into his teaching, and passion. Although, like an
actor, he had the skill to turn emotion on and off, it was genuine
nonetheless while he displayed it, generated out of the interaction
between text and interpreter. Certainly, he wore his heart on his sleeve,
but it was not a heart that bled uncontrollably. And this was what his
students, his audiences, responded to, because it made the subject-matter
real, vital, something to engage with. From my own experience, this is a
rare quality in a teacher, particularly a university teacher. Of those whom
I encountered in my many years at universities in New Zealand and
Germany, none could match this quality.

There were some who were perhaps more scholarly, but they had
wrung all the emotion out of their thoughts before imparting them to
us. There were others who performed and entertained, but who were
unable to give a coherent account of their topics. There were still others
who were bored, or lazy, or arrogant, or simply unimaginative. I am
unable to comment on the intellectual content of Arthur's teaching and
writing: I am not a Shakespearian or Miltonian scholar. Keith Sinclair, in

his history of Auckland University, says that Arthur was more of a literary critic than a scholar. I am not altogether sure what Sinclair means, but if it is the critic who brings an appreciation of and enthusiasm for art and literature to a wider audience, then perhaps the critic in Arthur did overshadow the scholar. On the other hand, there are the books on Shakespeare and Milton's Christian doctrine, and a pioneering study of Katherine Mansfield, to help assert his claim to be a scholar. In the end, the distinction is probably unimportant. What is important is the fact that in his prime he was able to combine the two roles to perfection, lending his teaching substance through the habits of scholarship.

III

It is not easy to identify the constellation of factors which made Arthur the person he was. I am always fascinated by brilliant individuals who spring from unlikely backgrounds. What is it that made my father, the third son of a pharmacist in a not particularly salubrious part of an obscure Humberside borough become an intellectual, a wit, and a man of the world?

If Arthur were alive today, he would be well into his nineties. Because he was already 47 when I was born, he always seemed to me to reach far back into history, and I used to think that he was, for example, a contemporary of Lord Nelson, even though there wasn't the vaguest hint of anything nautical about him. In fact, he was born in Goole, a town in Yorkshire, on 9 August 1903, so the First World War would have been at least a vivid memory for him. Indeed, his very proper eldest brother, Major, with whom he always had an uneasy relationship, served in the army during that war.

The most important early influence on Arthur, however, was not the Great War but the Methodist Church. The Sewell family were devout Methodists – to the letter, which meant that no alcohol, not even medicinal, crossed the threshold of the house at 16 Bridge Street, Goole. The impression of his childhood he always conveyed to me was of a severe and repressed household. The unfinished memoir which occupied him in his retirement does nothing to dispel that impression. Not only was there no alcohol in the house, there were almost no visitors. The voices of the six children – three boys and three girls – were always hushed, except when the family gathered around the piano to sing hymns; and there was, he claimed, 'nowhere for them to play'. From the age of seven he attended 'five religious sessions' every Sunday, and occasional weeknight services as well. But the neighbourhood, in spite of the presence of the Sewell household, had a profane ambience: five pubs were close by, and on Saturday night Arthur and his elder brother, Walter, could look down from their back bedroom onto Sewell's Yard and watch drunken women brawling. Also, if you were to believe Arthur, you would think that the Sewell children were underfed. But where did he learn to cook such traditional dishes as Yorkshire pudding, steak and kidney, and dumplings if not at home? And acquire the perverse taste for pigs' trotters, brawn, and tripe and onions?

I now know that he exaggerated the privations of his childhood. His sister, Gert, the sibling who was closest to him and who regarded herself as his 'moral mentor' and him as her 'intellectual mentor', put it all in perspective many years after his death. The truth was, she said, that the family ate extremely well, and there was lively conversation around the dining-room table – as often as not about politics, for they were ardent followers of the Liberal Party. And though their father, William John, was a tall, austere man, their mother, Ada Mary, was by all accounts a lovely, gentle little lady. It also seems that even the Methodist Church had a (limited) sense of fun. After week-night services there were recitals of secular pieces like Longfellow's 'Excelsior'. Arthur claimed that by taking part in such recitals he 'formed [his] lecturing style. [He] learned early how to play an audience with [his] hands and voice – and stuttering to gain time to remember or think.'

Whatever the truth, I understand now that it was the psychological effect more than the reality of the Methodist ethos in the family which oppressed him. To someone with a lively and mischievous mind it would have become stifling, to the extent that as an adult he would naturally cast his childhood in a more negative light than it deserved. It engendered in him a dislike of confinement of any kind and a restlessness which never really left him, even in his old age when it was illness that confined him.

Not all his siblings had the same reaction. Major became a pillar of the Chapel, as well as of society: he founded a chain of pharmacies and was elected an alderman of the City of Sheffield. Jo, his eldest sister, became a missionary in India and never married. Gert, so like him in her way of speaking and deadpan sense of humour, settled for the less rigorous demands of Anglicanism. I do not know about his youngest sister, Lil, who died young; but Walter, like Arthur, must have been something of a disappointment to his parents. He ended up as the proprietor of a small pharmacy in Saint Pancras, unmarried, a boarding-house dweller who drank and smoked too much. I have photographs of them all on my study wall: Gert and Arthur, she a baby still, he a perky toddler; Walter and Arthur, the young blades at the seaside, Arthur in a boater (ever the dandy); and all six of them, the three eldest at the front, with Arthur in the centre of the second row looking a little uncomfortable and out of place, twisting his body slightly to the side.

IV

There was a way out of his background, however: through education; and, whether by design or not, he took full advantage of it. He was a precocious little boy, a characteristic which in some respects never left him. His headmaster at Goole Grammar School, a Mr Forth, told him once that he was 'a small boy with a small boy's mind and an able boy's brain', a description which stung but was no doubt apt. He *was* small, and like many small men made up for it by exploiting a smart intellect and exercising a quick tongue. Certainly, they both got him into trouble, but they also helped him to win the necessary scholarships, first to grammar school, then to Leeds University, and finally to Queen's College, Oxford. He wanted to be a mathematician, but also studied English. English won in the end, but I am sure his mathematical bent helped him in the study of philosophy, giving him an analytical tool which would combine usefully with his emotional grasp of literature.

What I know of his university years is tied very closely to the development of his personality. For it was at both Leeds and Oxford that he perfected a number of defence mechanisms to deal with his modest (though not, I think, humble) background, his relative youth, his small stature, his lack of self-confidence, and the intense competition. He wrote that '[c]ompetition was for me keen, squalid, and various, and at all times I lied, bluffed, sulked, and cheeked my way to keep away from the last place in the rat race. There was no time, no desire for dedication to scholarship.' This must be an exaggeration, since he was too sharp to be anywhere near the bottom of the class, and I cannot imagine that it was possible to pass, and pass with some distinction, through underhand means alone the Leeds honours examinations. No doubt there was some element of bluff – there always is in academic study – but this was knowledge that was genuinely acquired, standing him in good stead as a teacher. I am prepared to believe much of the rest, however.

I can understand his situation. Not only was he small and 'common' (as the English upper middle classes so sneeringly put it), but he had bad acne, and his fellow-students were largely ex-officers from the War who had a life experience which he, with an upbringing he described as 'tantamount to house-arrest', could never share. In this situation his academic cleverness was less of an advantage. But he had another gift which provided, if not a solution, then a diversion. His recitals in chapel as a child had enhanced his skills as a performer. In his second year at Leeds he wrote and performed plays for the University Dramatic Society. Until the last few years of his career, when his energy gave out, he took part in readings, acted in plays, and directed highly successful productions. And, of course, there were his performances in the lecture hall. This acting gift allowed him, first, to shed his regional accent, to the extent that his normal speaking voice adopted a sonorous Oxford inflexion, although he could always lapse at will into those honest Yorkshire vowels which had so exposed him. Secondly, it allowed him to play roles, to pretend to be what he was not: in short, to lie imaginatively. His father was variously transformed into a doctor, a struck-off doctor (with the added fascination of that status), or the managing director of a chain of chemists' shops. He himself had been expelled from a minor public school for messing about with girls, for drinking, for cheating: take your pick. Apparently, he was not alone amongst his peers in resorting to such dissembling behaviour. He gives an insight into 'the practice of lying' in his memoir:

> . . . to tell exuberant or plainly silly lies has always come easily to me. I am not alone in this, but I wish it was the truth that came easily to me. I am forever a character, I am forever playing different parts, presenting myself variously according to the theatre and the part that I – part author, part actor – have a chance to play. The parts I play do not have to be related to reality. They do not have to be consistent. I can forget them as easily as I play them.

To me, this is one of the few occasions when he was utterly candid. Although he claims in the memoir not to be 'shooting lines', to be setting down 'a plain, unvarnished tale', he still postures: about his upbringing, for instance, or his cavalier attitude towards his university studies. None of that does any harm. It is impossible to resist a measure of embellishment in autobiography, in order to make a better story, to justify or avenge yourself in retrospect. And it is also understandable that often he was simply indulging his sense of fun at the expense of the pompous and gullible. Their gullibility encouraged him. More than that, he believed that gullibility is a 'moral offence. It transforms fancy into lies.'

But to his family and his friends, his disregard for the truth could be bewildering and hurtful. There was the time he agreed to play in the fathers' cricket match at my school. I now realise the notion was preposterous, at his age then, and state of fitness. But I waited and waited, and he did not turn up. Or the time he invited some friends to another friend's party, and then had to withdraw the invitation on the pretext that the host had taken a dislike to them. There were the stories he told my mother when he was unable to decide whether they were to have a life together.

But acting and lying helped him to survive in a difficult environment, and he emerged from Leeds with a first, and then from Oxford, where he would have us believe that he did no work, with a good second and appointment to a senior lectureship at Cape Town University. He was taught by some very distinguished scholars: by the poet Lascelles Abercrombie and J. R. R. Tolkien (who was apparently rather otherworldly) at Leeds; by C. S. Lewis and the philosopher Gilbert Ryle at Oxford. He maintained that he never took full advantage of his contact with these great men. One reason was that he cut lectures; another was his lack of confidence – he simply didn't feel clever enough to approach them on a more than superficial level. He was still the small boy with a small boy's mind, and, as he said, if he had 'any claim to cleverness, it took me by surprise after I was 30'. Nevertheless, something must have filtered through; he must have been sufficiently impressed by their scholarship to come to value good scholarship himself, and inspired enough to want to take up an academic career, however accidentally he seems to have fallen into it. It was a career which was to take him first to Cape Town, then to Auckland, Athens, Barcelona, Ankara, Beirut, and finally back to New Zealand, to Hamilton.

V

In spite of, and sometimes because of, his facility as a liar, Arthur was able to make and maintain numerous friendships throughout his life. He had a capacity for love, which extended, though not in any homoerotic way, to men as well as women. He could speak quite unselfconsciously about loving other men. I imagine that, like a southern European, he would have had no difficulty with embracing men. He was certainly a tender father, at least in my earliest years. He it was who took on most of the child-rearing duties, relieving my mother, who was slightly appalled by the messy and tedious business. He would bounce me on his knee to the jingle, 'What do they put in the sauce? – *Tar-tar!*' (dropping me suddenly and deliciously on the last syllable), or sing silly songs to me, such as (to the tune of 'Colonel Bogey'): 'Oh be kind to your friends in the swamp. / For the duck, as you know, had a mother. / Oh be kind to your friends in the swamp, / where the climate is awfully domp. / Oh you may think this song has an end. / So it has!' We also developed a nonsense language, which as I recall revolved largely around a word for 'chocolate'.

For some years, I reciprocated his warmth. For example, Arthur suffered terribly from inflamed sinuses, and I remember that sometimes, when he was driving me to school (I was always made to sit in the back, for reasons of safety), I would stroke his temples and forehead to ease the pressure and soothe the pain. However, by the age of 10, I began to shun any physical contact in our relationship. I think this disappointed him, and contributed to the distance that grew between us from then on. We never became friends, as such. Occasionally, we would have 'boys' outings', when he would take me to Beirut airport for breakfast or to La Fontana di Trevi (a fashionable Italian restaurant in Beirut) for a lasagne and a crème caramel. What we talked about then I hardly remember. I do recall him informing me during such an expedition, at a time when I was going through the usual pre-adolescent religious phase, that 'of course' he didn't believe in God. I was so impressed by his audacity that I more or less gave up religion on the spot. But perhaps on the whole I bored him. Small boys can be boring. He could bore me, too, particularly when he'd been drinking. I still regret the time I told him as much, over Christmas dinner towards the end of his life, when he was sick and depressed. The silence afterwards was palpable.

But I don't believe that many outside his immediate family were bored by him. That is one of the great discrepancies I have to reconcile, between the family view of him and the more public one. He was able to engage anyone in conversation – fellow academic, his doctor, a farm labourer in a pub, children – without condescension and quickly establish an easy rapport. As a non-academic friend of his wrote after his death:

> *He had a humanity; at the same time a humility which enabled him, even with his enormous scholarship, to mix with anyone freely whatever their station. I think he is the one person in my life in fact who commanded my admiration for one thing too – I never, as long as I knew him, heard him talk down to anyone.*

My cousins to this day recall the way he would entertain them with silly, long-winded stories which depended for their humour on sustaining the tension of the absurdity and on timing. A favourite was one about a talking pigeon which becomes the toast of London society. But enduring friendships would also develop out of such contact. I cannot list all his special friends, let alone describe them: there are so many parts of his life which remain mysterious to me. But a few names come to the surface, one way or another. Dick Anschutz, the philosopher; Willis Airey, a much loved historian; and Rex Fairburn – above all Rex – at Auckland. Louis MacNeice; David King, my godfather; and George Katsimbalis (immortalised by Henry Miller and Lawrence Durrell) in Athens. Dan Davin, Arthur's publisher, at Oxford. Roland Puccetti, a much younger American, in Beirut.

Of these, only two made any real impact on me. Of Arthur's relationship with Rex, regrettably little seems to survive but inscribed first editions of *Strange Rendezvous* and *The Sky is a Limpet*, and a sentence in a letter of Rex's of 6 November 1937 to Denis Glover, which states simply: 'I miss Sewell.' (*The Letters of A. R. D. Fairburn*, 1981). Their relationship was, I believe, a very male one, but without the usual undertones of violence – a contest in hilarity, in which they would swap 'outrageous propositions' and even converse in rhyming couplets. It is a relationship from which I am entirely excluded, even as a spectator. But I do remember Louis, and that long, melancholic face of his, from when we stayed in his house near Regent's Park in the early 1960s. Louis died suddenly in 1963. Arthur wept openly. I was appalled:

grown men didn't cry, especially not over the loss of a mere friend.

Not only could he weep at the death of a friend; he could write a poem about him:

In Memory: Louis MacNeice

Not smiling, remote and intimate,
You came into our bedroom (bringing us the Times, *I think).*
Then, you would look out over Regent's Park
Pondering, although it had little to do with us,
How fearful the leap into the daylight from the dark.

Not all that dark, perhaps: it was the twilight of a day
(We didn't know how soon the hour would come).
You wanted full and unabated daylight
To excite again − why not? − those membranes then grown numb.
You were fifty-five and, as men are used to say,
Fifty-five is by no means the end of the day.

It was the end of yours. What struck you, I suppose the doctors know.
You died (as something in you lived) by the book.
You sought life, too, as a bookish man might do,
Your pint of Guinness would froth into a poem.
And now no more shall we, loving you as we did,
Listen to your silences, and wonder
What shy criticisms in those silences you hid.

I'm sorry that Arthur didn't write more poetry. A handful of poems survive: this one comes closest to catching his speech rhythms, with the variation in syntax, the asides. And it catches something of Louis, too, his distance, and the lonely melancholy of the poet in a dry period.

Although I have not seen Roland Puccetti for some 30 years, he is nevertheless the friend of Arthur's whom I recall most clearly. The age difference would have been at least 20 years: Arthur, a product of the British academic system, nearing the end of his career; and Roland, a product of the North American one, beginning to make his way towards professorships in Singapore and Canada. Roland would come up in the afternoon to our house in the hills above Beirut for drinks that might often flow into dinner. In summer we would sit outside, on the front porch or under an enormous fig-tree, as the light faded, the roar of the cicadas intensified, and the fruit bats began crashing in and out of the foliage. They drank cheap Lebanese red wine (Ksara) or the local beer (Almaza or Laziza) or perhaps the whisky or gin which never improved Arthur's disposition, and they talked and laughed without restraint, Arthur play-acting, gossiping, pontificating, spreading warmth. I was only a child, an onlooker, but even now I regard such alfresco conviviality as the best way to enjoy life.

Arthur not only entertained and inspired Roland, but would also have been something of a mentor – even if it was only to persuade him not to take academic pretensions and competitiveness too seriously. To Roland it was a pivotal friendship: after Arthur's death Roland wrote a tribute containing two very simple statements which I count among the most complimentary of all. 'Reading the obituaries,' he said, 'made me feel like someone who got on a wonderful train or ship between one stop or port and another . . . and who wishes he could have gotten on earlier and stayed on until the end of the voyage.' More simply, he also wrote: 'He was just one of those people I would rather have around, and now cannot have around, most of the time.' There is an unintended ambiguity about the second sentence which I particularly like. Because if Roland is still alive, a part of Arthur must be around him still.

In later years, after his return to New Zealand, Arthur reserved his conviviality for the pub – the rather stark and furtive pubs of the 1960s. The house remained quiet. As he grew frailer, the trips to the pub became less and less frequent; and when he did go, it was often followed by several days in bed or confined to his living room chair. His brothers Walter and Major and his old friends and contemporaries were dying one by one. He took the deaths of Willis Airey and R. A. K. Mason, for instance, as something of a personal assault. They not only made him more aware of his own mortality; they increased his sense of isolation. Memories are a poor substitute for dead friends.

VI

If men could succumb to Arthur's charm, women – colleagues, colleagues' wives, students, shop assistants, secretaries, nurses – seemed all the more susceptible. He was married twice, which in retrospect doesn't surprise me. In fact, it seems a modest number of wives for such a man. It did surprise me as a 10 year-old, though, when my mother disclosed that he had been married before: only *other* people's parents got divorced and remarried. His first wife, Peggy, was a Jewish South African, and he married her in 1929 when he was relatively young. She is described by those who knew her as being tall, elegant ('a Pre-Raphaelite style of beauty,' someone said), and rather reserved. Nobody seems to speak negatively about her, except Arthur. He brought her to New Zealand in 1933, and by the time he left in 1945 the marriage was over, although it flickered briefly into life again in the following year. What drove them apart was a difference in values and also the appearance of my mother, Rosemary Seymour, on the scene.

I suspect that where Arthur had a certain disdain for the social niceties, and lacked much sense of property, to Peggy both were important. She tried to make him into something he was not, and increasingly the contradictions became too extreme. She was also probably no intellectual match for him. My mother, on the other hand, was more than his intellectual match, though perhaps without his flair, and she was if anything even more contemptuous of the social niceties than Arthur was; and although she did have a sense of property, it was hardly orthodox. In addition, she was young and beautiful when their relationship ignited, and one of his students. Nowadays, affairs between professor and student are not tolerated because of the power imbalance which they imply. But from what I know of Arthur and my mother, I find it difficult to accept that there was any element of exploitation in their relationship: she was too tough, intellectually and emotionally.

I am unable to reconstruct fully the course of my parents' relationship, or the chain of events which led eventually to their marriage in 1951. The record is fragmentary – just a few tantalising letters – and not only the protagonists but also those in most of the supporting roles are dead. I am not entirely sorry that so much remains obscure: it gives me less opportunity to pry into their privacy. I do not know the circumstances of their first encounter, but it could have been as early as 1938, when my mother went up to Auckland University College. By the beginning of 1945, an intimate relationship had most definitely developed. Sometime during that year, things got nasty at the university – a sanctimonious faction on the Council put pressure on Arthur – and the following year he was back in England, without my mother and without employment. The reasons for his return to England are more complex and more interesting than this bare account suggests, however.

For one thing, he was running away – panicked by the enormity of the social outrage he had perpetrated. Not only its local impact would have been responsible for this: one has to remember the moral code imposed on him by his early upbringing, something he could never totally erase. He also felt guilty at the suffering which he had caused Peggy, who returned to South Africa to try and salvage something from her life. These feelings were expressed in an undated letter to his sister, Gert, written from Marseilles on his way to Athens in 1946:

> . . . coming to England had a strange effect on me. I felt that I had missed the war and that I had been during all the horror adding to the spiritual chaos of the world by this affair which, through breaking up marriage, broke also something of the general order of the world. I still wanted Rosemary, but even more I wanted to be of some social use in life.

What is particularly interesting about this passage is that he speaks of his own situation as he would of the situation of a tragic hero who also disrupts 'the general order of the world' and pays for it, usually with his life. In Arthur's case, the punishment was not so severe. But, after leaving Auckland, there followed a long period of insecurity, loneliness, and reassessment.

He was offered a position in 1946 as Byron Professor of English at Athens University, a position that paid well but which, apart from some public lectures, had no formal teaching duties. Instead of simply enjoying the privileges – something it was very much in his nature to do – he set about transforming the job into a teaching position. He managed this by establishing a reputation through his public lectures, and also through giving informal classes; in addition, he cajoled the authorities, both Greek and British, into supporting his efforts. So he was, after all, given an opportunity to 'be of some social use' and redeem himself in the eyes of the gods; and what more appropriate place to achieve this than Greece?

Greece had a healing effect on him in other ways. It inspired in him a new humility and allowed him to sort out his priorities at last. The most important of these was his need to be with my mother once again. This was probably no straightforward matter, however. It was the direct aftermath of the Second World War: travel was restricted; travel documents and permits difficult to obtain. My parents had to endure a long period of separation; first, while Arthur made up his mind; and, secondly, while arrangements were made to get her to Athens. In the meantime, they corresponded; or at least Arthur corresponded, because no letters from my mother survive. His few extant letters are a wonderful mixture of passion, description, and intellectual dialogue. One opens straight into a discussion of the playwright John Ford, on whom my mother was then writing a thesis in London.

But another, written in diary form during a three-day stay on the island of Aegina just before Easter in (I think) 1947, brings to life something of the drama of my parents' relationship and Arthur's state of mind:

Aegina. Sunday: March 23

Darling heart, I am on an island where no-one seems to speak English except myself and I am to be here for three days – it will be a most unusual thing for me to keep virtually silent for so long . . . I am alone on this farm and I shall do some drawings of it for you. You must please tell me the moment you are tired of my drawings. Then I won't do any more for you.

I have already broken the seat of the WC – but I fancy it was only pinned together – and the lampglass – because I trimmed it too high too soon.

You are on the mantelpiece – twice.

The light is too dim to read by and I am writing this with some difficulty: but you can almost hear the silence behind all the country noise, such is the change from the everlasting row of Athens. . . . Aegina has a positive silence – as positive as the silence I feel because you are not here. Do you ever feel the absence of someone – I mean of me – as a silence? I often feel your absence like that – not that you are allowed to be very talkative when you are with me, are you? Sweetheart, when you're very down and in the dumps, do you think it might help you to think how good it will be to talk again? I haven't really talked (I've lectured, of course) since I left you. I often have a daydream of walking with you (not, perhaps, to Stoke Poges) as I used to, and of talking to you. I also want to hear you Huh! as only you can . . .

This is the hell of a light! I shall go to bed very early and read by candlelight. . .

Monday morning

Darling, I have just had my breakfast and shall shortly set out to the village of Aegina, with my pencil and my sketchbook, and perhaps a book of A.E. Coppard's short stories . . .

The birds woke me, but not only the birds. Next door to this farm, living in an enormous chateau kind of villa, is Mrs Londou's half-aunt [Mrs Londou was Arthur's landlady in Athens], a poor mad woman, who calls out, especially at daybreak, in any one of six languages. She is kept here with two nurses, but she comes out on the balcony in her dressing gown, and shouts what must be curses across the Mediterranean. They locked her up, poor thing, after a distressing episode when her husband was ambassador in Paris, many years ago. She came downstairs to a reception wearing nothing but a fur coat. Most of the day, I fancy, they give her drugs and she is quite quiet.

Tonight, if I can, I shall put my mind to Ford, darling . . .

And now, darling heart, I'm going to sleep for a little while – say, until three o'clock or so, when I shall do another drawing for you. Tell me when to stop, won't you?

Later.

I didn't sleep. I lay in the sun and I don't doubt that I shall be sunburnt. As I was lying there, I had the curious physical illusion of Time slipping by over me with the clouds, and I didn't at all like it. It occurred to me, although why I shouldn't imagine, that Mr Churchill is over 70, Harold Nicholson (why Harold Nicholson? I don't know) over 60, and Professor Forder 57. For my own part, with all the concessions in the world, I am 43 . . .

There is more: in fact, 14 pages altogether, in the neat but not easily legible hand affected by so many of his generation. He describes his simple Greek meals and how (unusually for him) he relishes them; how he is briefly arrested by the army while sketching a view; and how he mistakes an ordinary dwelling for a taverna and is nevertheless offered *retsina*, olives, and a hunk of bread, for which payment is refused. But what makes this letter so valuable to me is that it encapsulates so much of Arthur's personality and of his relationship with my mother. He was, for instance, accident-prone, in a benign way, getting himself into awkward situations which he was nevertheless able to get out of

ARTHUR
SEWELL

through his charm and a kind of innocence or even obliviousness. He was talkative and impossible to compete with when in full flight. His conversation would flow from entertaining anecdote into philosophical musing into literary argument. He also needed bringing down to earth – and my mother, 16 years younger and much less given to fancy, was just the person to do it ('Huh!'). I don't know the exact state of their relationship when this letter was written, but there is a sense that my mother was not responding as Arthur wanted. There is an impatience, an urgency. Hence the reference to time – and his life – slipping by. And as I write this, I am aware that when he wrote this letter Arthur was a year younger than I am today and already had his most productive years behind him.

There is also a happy ending to the story. My mother joined Arthur in Athens in 1947, and lived in an adjoining flat with his landlady; but they didn't marry until 1951, and then only after I – much to everyone's surprise – was conceived. The story of their wedding is as remarkable as the course of their relationship up to that time. Arthur was very nearly married to Winnie Davin, one of the wedding party, because she was the only one wearing a hat. They had to borrow a wedding ring at the ceremony, and it was returned to its owner in full view of the (already bemused) Kensington Registrar. The bride and groom then went their separate ways because they had separate business to attend to. The registrar – who had admonished the divorced Arthur before the ceremony by saying, 'You realise, Professor, that marriage is for life!' – was left wondering what marital irregularity he had been a party to. But the marriage endured for over 20 years, until Arthur's death.

VII

I know Arthur much better now, 24 years after his death. I have grown up a little in the meantime, and I have spent many hours thinking about him. I also feel that I have a more solid relationship with him than I ever had while he was alive. I am more relaxed about his weaknesses and more admiring of his achievements. Of course, he is not here to irritate or embarrass or bore me. But that is not the whole explanation. The major difference between my attitude towards him then and now is that I have a clearer insight into his pain: not so much the physical pain caused by the cancer that smouldered inside him, but the mental pain, the inner conflicts, the disappointments, the slights, the dismay at getting old, and the fear of dying.

It has been a long process. For many years I had a recurring dream, in which he would appear, not dramatically, like the ghost of Hamlet's father, but in a very matter-of-fact way: perhaps at a party we had both been invited to, or in the kitchen. There was enormous frustration for me in these meetings because in the dream we never connected: he would simply look at me in a severe, disappointed way, or I would be disapproving of his behaviour; then I would wake up or drift on, as one so often does, to another, inconsequential dream. This poem, written at a long interval after his death, expresses something of my frustration:

Twelve Years Dead

Again last night. Never on the dot, nor
winding me into neurosis. Not even regular,
like the Friday beer at the pub. Just
the infrequent visitation, reminding me
not to forget.
         Nothing had changed
(why should it?): a small bottle of whisky
amongst the groceries. It does me good
you know. *I suppose it did. Sometimes*
I tell myself we would have drunk
together, talking philosophy amongst men.

But then I never was one to understand
abstractions or vague promises. You were

someone I learnt early not to rely on,
as I waited yet again after school.
(FROM *MAKING THE FAR LAND GLOW*, 1986)

He was, I believe, at least an incipient alcoholic. He had a tendency to gulp, rather than sip, alcohol, and there were periods in his life when I have no doubt that he used alcohol to suppress a sense of failure. Alcohol helped him to contemplate less fearfully his awareness of the decline in his powers and in his influence, as he moved further and further away in time from his Auckland heyday. I more than once surprised him helping himself to an illicit glass of gin or whisky, and he would implore me not to tell my mother. Sometimes I did, for which he would reproach me as one schoolboy would another: 'You little sneak!' I dare say I was. The poem, then, reflects his problem with alcohol. It also reflects the fact that he wasn't much good as a father in that state, and that any genuine connection was unlikely.

These dreams petered out – as did another recurring dream of mine about being back at school, with an adult sensibility in a small boy's body. But an anger persisted, an anger that Arthur had always been too old to be a proper father; an anger that he had never instructed me in physical skills like sport and woodwork, as fathers are supposed to; an anger that I never seem to have absorbed even his intellectual skills; an anger, in short, that I had missed out. This anger was never very healthy, because there was no outlet for it, and there is nothing a dead parent can do to meet that anger. But then came a final dream which dispelled it for good. My recall of the detail is hazy. We were travelling in a bus in a European city – possibly in the Netherlands, because I have a picture of neatly planted beds of bright red and yellow tulips. He was seated in the row in front of me. Suddenly, he turned round to face me . . . That is all; but it is enough. The connection had been made finally; the anger was gone.

Of course, one way or another he did pass on some of his skills while he was alive. Once I asked him to look at a rather bad essay of mine on *King Lear* which I felt had been unfairly graded. Arthur responded with eight pages of comments, ending with the advice:

Bill: I have been deliberately harsh. You seem to have thought English is much easier than it really is. Be yourself ruthlessly self-critical for a month

or so. Avoid purple patches. Stick rigorously to the point. Avoid general
remarks. Feel the effect of character, language and situation. Be concrete.

He was quite right. It is a habit of mine to think that any discipline is
easier than it is, and to abandon it as soon as I meet any resistance. Self-
criticism is not something I practise with particular rigour: he should
have suggested not the period of 'a month or so', but a whole lifetime
in which to be 'ruthlessly self-critical'. But in my own writing I do try
to follow his simple instructions: not to overembellish, or wander from
the point, or make a general remark without substantiating it.

VIII

I missed Arthur's death. I was in another city; and though he had been
in poor health for some years, he had shown no particular signs of
dying. As my mother wrote some years later, 'Arthur had no intention
of dying so soon.' Of course, no one intends to die before they are ready;
but people in retirement do often let go. Arthur had by no means
finished with life. He very much wanted to finish the memoir. There is
so much about his 12 productive years in Auckland, for instance, which
is missing from it: his teaching, his political activities, his relationship
with my mother (perhaps), and his friendship and contact with so many
of the intellectuals and artists of the period. But I think the volume of
research and writing that doing justice to the Auckland years would have
demanded daunted him both physically and mentally. There would also
have been an emotional barrier to confront, the fact that after Auckland
his career started to decline. He kept putting the job off, and then it was
too late.

The first chapter of the memoir opens with the sentence, 'The home
in which I was born was very different from the home in which I am
dying'; it concludes, 'It is November, 1969, and when the examination
papers are all marked, I shall have done with teaching the young. For the
rest of my dying.' You might think that these words show a certain
preparedness for death. Yet in the same chapter he protests, 'I have a
certain smell about me of mortality, but I do not think I am ripe or
ready'. The truth is that he used – though not in any dishonest manner
– his final illness and the conclusion it held out towards him as yet

another of his roles, one he had learned to play from his vast knowledge
of the poets and philosophers:

Death though was something he comprehended
only from the literature, a role he could shrug
off, get up from, something about which immortal words
(ripeness, be absolute, silence) *had been spoken,*
but he never believed them —
                    I'm sick as a dog,
he would say. And make his plans for tomorrow.
(FROM *MAKING THE FAR LAND GLOW*)

It is ironic, then, that when he did die he made no grand exit, with
family and friends hushed, around his bedside. There were no significant
or mysterious last words. There wasn't even a dash to hospital or the
indignity of being on life support. His lungs filled with fluid and he just
slipped away one morning while my mother was doing the dishes next
door.

I don't know if this is what he or the poets and philosophers would
have thought of as an appropriate departure. What I do know is that if
you are unsure of what awaits you after death, and if an early devout
upbringing leaves you with a certain ambivalence towards the afterlife,
then to keep on making plans for tomorrow — in spite of the imminence
of death — is not the worst way of being absolute for it. It was the last
lesson he taught, and though I missed his death, I don't think I have
missed the point of that lesson.

An Ordinary and Decent Man

Tony Simpson on *Harry Simpson*

I cannot open a packet of fish and chips without it evoking one of my two earliest memories of my father. The waft of fish in batter, vinegar, and warmed newsprint instantly conjures a midday scene on the bank of the Avon River in Christchurch, looking across at what was then the band rotunda. My father, a thickset man with dark wavy hair and the deeply tanned face of someone who has spent many years of his working life in the open air, is dressed in a grey shirt and grease-stained khaki overalls. He is laughing about something that my mother has said. It must be 1949: I started school in 1950, and this was an ordinary working day. The previous year we had moved to Christchurch from Rangiora, where I was born in 1945.

What were we doing there? In the immediate sense it doesn't matter, but I think that in the broader sense we were comforting my mother. Over the previous 20 years my family had been following a common economic pattern. As the economy had capitalised and the widespread need for manual labour had declined, my father had been forced to leave the West Coast where he had worked since his marriage sometime in the 1920s. Timber workers were no longer required in numbers, and so he and my mother had packed up and gone to Rangiora in North Canterbury, where her parents lived. Our family spent the Depression, the post-Depression period, and the Second World War and its immediate aftermath there. My father did a variety of jobs, one of which involved him driving the local taxi and doubling as a night-shift hearse driver if required. When I was a child, he could sometimes be induced to tell stories full of black humour about this. Eventually he ended up as what was known back then as an 'oiler and greaser' in a garage. I have no idea if this occupation still exists.

In Rangiora, my mother kept many hundreds of hens. Another early childhood memory is of the dusty, foetid smell of a summer hen run. From the proceeds of selling the eggs she bought our first house, a bone of contention between my parents for many years. Her sense of the roles to be played by husband and wife was very strong, acute, and black-and-white. In her estimation, his was the role of provider. If it was she who had bought a house, then that was an indication of a fundamental gap in the performance of his role, a failure for which she was entitled to upbraid him.

The logic of the changing economy – the same logic which brought thousands of Maori to the cities in the same period – and the educational needs of my older brothers drove our family to move again, this time to Christchurch. There my father found a job similar to the one in Rangiora in a central city garage. My mother didn't find the move easy. For something over a decade she had lived in the town where she had grown up, and where her parents (and then her widowed mother) continued to live. Now she was living in a suburb in a strange city without the ready access to support of family and friends to which she was used. She had a small and active preschool child to look after, besides three older sons and a husband. Christchurch can be an unwelcoming and socially impenetrable place for newcomers, who can't be placed by a dozen important criteria, and more particularly by the school they had attended. It was also a place that quite rigidly defined families by the occupation of the husband. In Rangiora, my mother had been the daughter of William Shilton, watchmaker and jeweller; in Christchurch she was the wife of Harry Simpson, oiler and greaser. To her the move to Christchurch meant a downward change in her social status which she found very hard to tolerate and resented deeply.

These facts have determined almost the whole of my subsequent relationship with my father since, or at least as far as I can puzzle it out. On the particular day of the fish and chips, I suspect that my mother, very lonely and unhappy, had taken the bus into town to have lunch with my father so that she might at least get through the day without lapsing into the tearful melancholy that social psychologists – looking for a label to hang on a widespread phenomenon so that it could be safely filed away and ignored – would later call 'suburban neurosis'. Of course, I don't know if the trip to town helped my mother. I wasn't even aware of that dimension of the experience at the time. Instead, it lodged firmly in my mind as a day of unusual excitements. Small boys love to see their fathers in their place of work, to imbibe its smells and colours and rhythms. They enjoy in particular the relationship they can have through their own father with the other men in the workplace, the joking about incomprehensible things in which boy and father and workmates are somehow intimately involved. Eating fish and chips in the sun on the banks of a river afterwards turned the day into sheer heaven, and certainly one to remember.

My other very early memory of my father is to do with books. This memory is set at home, also in 1949, and for some reason my father is late. I know this because it is dark and he has not eaten with us. This was unusual. We always ate as a family with 3ZB going on the radio. All his life, too, he cultivated the habit of going to work early and coming home in the late afternoon if possible. Curiously, this is a working pattern which I also have fallen into over the last decade, as have my surviving brothers; perhaps there is a genetic disposition to these things. Probably my father had been working overtime, and it was dark because it was winter. He can't have been to the pub, because at that stage of his life he didn't drink. But this is all background to the main reason why the moment stands out in my recollection. When he finally arrived, he had brought me a book. I forget the title, but it was the first I had ever owned. And he said: 'When you've read this one, I'll buy you another.'

I don't know who taught me to read but I do know that I could read before I went to school, and that I could also read before the moment I have just described, although whether my father knew that I don't recall. I suspect that one of my brothers, who was also a precocious reader, had taught me, at least by example. But from that moment a pattern was established in my life. Since then, I have never been without at least one book which I am reading, and usually several. When I have finished one, I buy myself another.

Again, what induced my father to take this step I don't know. He wasn't educated in the formal sense. On the contrary, his schooling had ceased when he was 13. I have a studio portrait photograph of him – the only one that I own – at that moment, dressed in his first adult suit, as was then customary. The next working day he started at the Blackball mine, and he never stopped working until the day, over 50 years later, when he had the heart attack which ultimately would lead to his death. Of course, in his working life he learned many practical things, some of them sophisticated skills to do with mining or felling timber, and others more mundane but useful such as how to cobble boots or cut hair. Others were more esoteric such as how to lay the odds so that you came out winning if you were running a book, or now virtually obsolete practices, such as how to mould potatoes. Some of these skills he passed on to me: I can mould potatoes with the best of them, although I regret to say I don't know how to run a book. But he had no formal education after he left school. Reading is an activity I associate with him in memory only rarely, and then at a later period. I have no recollection whatever of him ever writing anything, not even a shopping list, and certainly not a letter; these things he left to my mother. Nevertheless, from somewhere or other he had picked up the notion that it was important that his children should be able to read fluently, and he had, with deliberation, set out to encourage us.

This is doubly curious in a way, although recently I think I may have stumbled across a part of the answer at least. Not only was he not a reader himself, but completing his schooling during the First World War meant that my father grew up in a world in which all of the adults with whom he associated were Victorians. Many of them would have been British immigrants, including his paternal grandfather Isaac, who had come to Nelson in 1843 and who lived with my father's parents for the last years of his life. Many of the attitudes my father held were much more typical of that immigrant era than of a later time. In particular, they reflect a family tradition of sorts. Isaac, who had been a farmer, had married the daughter of an original Nelson immigrant and cabin passenger named Patchett. During the course of the long voyage to New Zealand these passengers set up a debating society, according to the subsequently published account of one of their number, Alfred Fell. Over the two Thursdays of 4 and 11 November 1842, they debated the then highly topical issue, 'Is the education of the working classes beneficial to the general interests of the community?' 'I need scarcely say,' records Fell, 'that as a good Tory I gave my opinion against education.' But Patchett, 'who is a regular Radical', spoke strongly in favour.

This issue subsequently became the focus of significant debate within the settlement of Nelson where it was settled in favour of the radicals. Not only that, but in the 1870s, with the abolition of the provinces and

HARRY SIMPSON AT 14

the subsequent creation of a national education system, the egalitarian Nelson model was adopted for the whole country, a system which survived until the adoption of the Tomorrow's Schools report just a few years ago. I like, therefore, to see a family and community tradition at work in the actions of my father in buying me a book and promising more in an attempt – successful, as it transpired – to ensure that I became a lifelong reader.

The timing of my father's birth, in Collingwood in December 1903, had other consequences for our relationship. I was the last of four children, late child of a late and second marriage, so that he was older than the fathers of my playmates and contemporaries. Too young to go to the First World War, too old and with too many children to be conscripted for the Second, and perhaps too prudent to volunteer, he had not shared the experience of the majority of fathers during my childhood. When the children of these men retailed at second hand, and no doubt with considerable embroidery, the wartime experiences of their fathers, I was constrained to remain silent.

Being born in the first decade of the century also meant that my father had grown up during a period of vigorous anti-war agitation and union militancy. He was always sceptical about the value of military service and contemptuous of those who were enthusiastic about their wartime experience. These attitudes rubbed off on me and subsequently got me into trouble more than once in the days of compulsory cadet training in high school and adult military conscription.

That I have also been an active unionist all my life I attribute to my father's influence. Just before I left for my first real day at work (as a student, on the Lyttelton wharf) he took me aside and gave me the only two pieces of parental advice I ever had from him: 'No-one is indispensable,' he said, 'so never assume that the boss needs you', and

'Join the union'. Subsequent experience has confirmed the validity of this advice. I like to think that these things run as traditions in families, too. My father was never a union leader (although in line with his own advice, he was always a member), but my maternal great-uncle led the Wellington watersiders in the 1913 general strike.

All of these are positive things that stand out in my childhood relationship with my father, but everyone has a life of light and shade. Perhaps above all, the timing of my father's birth meant that he grew up prior to the First World War in a world in which such technologies as the internal combustion engine, electricity, and the telephone were rarities, and heavier-than-air flight was unheard of or regarded at best as an eccentricity. By the time of his death the world had convulsed itself in two terrible bloodlettings which shattered many beliefs and expectations. In the year in which he died there were men on the moon. My father found that the world to which he had been socialised kept dissolving and reforming, and he must have found this difficult both to cope with and to comprehend, although it was he himself who first drew to my attention the extent of the changes he had experienced in his life. I've remarked on what this meant in terms of his working life, and the need to uproot himself and his family at regular intervals. It also had considerable impact on his personal life, and thereby on mine.

Families, although they are fairly robust institutions, can break down under pressure. There were unusual pressures in our situation. I've already alluded to the loneliness and unhappiness of my mother, living in alienating circumstances in Christchurch in the 1950s, but the problems ran deeper than that. My mother always felt that she had missed life's chances. As the daughter of a small business proprietor, her marriage to a working man, in the teeth of strenuous parental opposition, was possibly the only serious act of social rebellion in her entire life. It was one that she almost instantly regretted. Egged on by her mother, she turned her marriage into a battleground where my father was always to blame for everything and anything. The source of her problems was general social change, but she was not to know and never to comprehend that. All she knew was that it had not turned out at all as she had expected and she had the answer right in front of her: it was him.

What strikes me in retrospect was my father's forbearance. This is not to say that he was never exasperated, nor impatient, nor furious. He was often all three, but he rarely allowed his temper to betray him. One of the things I value most is learning from him that humour is the sharpest of all social weapons. My general recollection of him is of a jolly man who laughed a great deal. As behoved someone who was once, according to family tradition – long before my birth, and perhaps uniquely in the annals of New Zealand law – convicted of being drunk in charge of a wheelbarrow, much of this laughter was at the expense of human folly.

In a period when it was accepted as axiomatic that one disciplined one's children by hitting them, and that this was largely the prerogative of fathers, I don't recall that he ever struck me. I was outraged when I went to school and discovered not only that this was allowed but that I was liable to have it applied to me for quite arbitrary reasons, a revelation to which I partly attribute my lifelong quarrel with authority and oppressive government. In fact I only witnessed violence from him once. Curiously, this was over me.

A brother of my mother's came to stay with us temporarily when I was, perhaps, seven years old, and my next oldest brother 14. This uncle had been thrown out by his wife: I don't know what for but in retrospect I have my suspicions. Certainly what was then darkly referred to as 'the booze' was involved. He had not been in our house for very long before he began to interfere sexually with both my brother and myself. Such things were much commoner then than is generally admitted, as any male child who grew up in that era will know if they are honest with themselves. I don't know how my father discovered what was happening but he did, and his response was short and sharp. My uncle left within the hour, nursing his bruises. Perhaps because this gave me the comfort of knowing that my father was my protector, I was particularly bereft when he left us when I was about 12. I quite literally didn't see him again for five years, notwithstanding that he continued to live in the same city and work in the same job.

These are crucial years in the life of any child and I blamed his absence for a great deal of what was simply growing up. In retrospect I hope that if I am not wiser about his motives I can, at least, see the broader picture. I think now that he was worn down by my mother's continual targeting of what she saw as his failure to deliver her due, and that he just walked away from it. To be fair to her, once he was gone and she was obliged to confront herself, she discovered some personal strengths that she never suspected she had, and from these built a much more rounded identity, so much so that five years on she felt able to invite my father to return. This he did and I had his company for two further years before I in my turn left home, married, and moved to another city.

But I was devastated by the betrayal I saw in his leaving and it made our relationship through those two years very difficult. This was not helped by those years coinciding with my first at university. Like many men of his time, my father, despite his lifelong commitment to the importance of education, was suspicious of universities: he perceived them as the bastions of privilege they had been until the Labour governments he always supported had opened them to working-class talent. The ambivalence he felt about this expressed itself as a simultaneous pride in my achievement, and an open hostility to everything that the university represented. I found this very hard to take while I was trying to get to know him again and to deal with the transition to the new world I had entered. One of my older brothers, who had also made this transition, although by a less direct route, and who might have assisted me, was not available to do so. As a cohesive unit our family had been irrevocably damaged by my father's absence.

It is instructive to observe how my siblings coped with all of this. The two eldest simply shut themselves off from it all and we rarely saw them. One joined a profession which took him away from Christchurch and eventually to another country. I have not spoken to him or communicated with him for over two decades. This has not been deliberate – I think that we simply drew opposite conclusions from our childhood experiences and we have nothing to say to one another. Another brother took the opportunity of our mother's death to dispose of most of the family records, including many photographs; hence my possession of only one photograph of my father. Perhaps most interesting and closest to my own response was that of the brother nearest to me in age, the one with whom I had shared the bewildering experience of childhood sexual abuse, with whom alone I could speak of that matter, and who is now dead. The last few years of his life were spent in an energetic search for the fugitive physical record of our family. It was he who located our great-grandfather's grave, and who discovered the reasons why our family had come to Australia and then to New Zealand (to buy horses for the Indian army), and why they had remained (great-grandfather Isaac's marriage). Gradually, and with great tenacity,

TONY SIMPSON
AGED FOUR

he tracked down and copied most of the documentary record of births, marriages and deaths which are the bare framework of the history of a family, passing these on to me as he went.

My life, too, has been partly spent in a search for our family, but a search of a less immediate and concrete sort. As it has emerged, it has been an attempt to find out what sort of man my father was, and what living in New Zealand meant to him. The person I have found was an ordinary, decent man, who worked hard, did his best, and made little mark, but who believed all his life that not just he but everyone was entitled to live decently and securely, in a community that had dedicated itself to that fundamental objective. He never articulated that but, in common with most of his contemporaries, simply lived it as axiomatic.

All of that discovery, and all that has been written here, has had to have its coherence invented; to be laboriously recollected, and painstakingly assembled, not just for this piece but also over the 29 years which have elapsed since my father died. In 1968, he had the first of a series of heart attacks which destroyed his mind, and a year later he was gone. In all, I knew him intimately for only 15 years of my life, most of that as a child. My last clear memory of him as the man I knew was of him holding my newborn son in his arms, his face beaming with delight.

Almost everything I have written since his death has been, in one way or another, and whatever else it might be, a part evocation of him. One of my great frustrations with the gradual development of my perception of my father, and what he meant to me, is that I have been unable, as others can with their still-living fathers, to check back on the validity of what I have been able to recreate of him. Two years ago, I think that I finally achieved the full evocation.

In June 1995, I went to Geneva to speak as representative of 20 public sector unions from various countries at an International Labour

Organisation conference on the process of public sector structural adjustment. This was by no means the first time I had spoken to an international gathering, but on this occasion I had a special responsibility. Much attention has been focused on New Zealand; in the international debates on this subject our experience is of particular relevance and is much lauded on the right of the political spectrum. Somehow, in the space of less than 20 minutes, I had to convey to this international gathering the sense that this was not the case, and that whatever might be claimed for the economic outcomes of the process, the social outcomes had been a disaster. I had to do this alone, in the face of a forbidding New Zealand government presence, and in front of several hundred delegates, both union and official. I feared that I would fail. Then, quite unbidden, I thought of my father, and everything he represented in the life he had lived, and how proud of me he would have been at that moment when I was defending before an international audience what his life had stood for. And in that instant I was no longer afraid. I don't know if I was successful or not in conveying my message to the Geneva audience. I do know that it annoyed the principal official New Zealand representative sufficiently for him to launch into a furious attempted rebuttal at the first available opportunity. That is neither here nor there. What it really signified for me was journey's end, because it seemed to me that my father and I, through that moment, had reached an understanding of one another at last.

PERFECTION AND A
NAGGING CURIOSITY

APIRANA TAYLOR on *MELVIN TAYLOR*

Thoughts of mortality well up within me as I think of my father whom I have brought into the hospital for his check-up. He is not well. My thoughts on death are followed by speculations on life and immortality. Is there something beyond this life? I wonder if the truths we find in art speak of immortality and whether or not art is like a gateway pointing to some higher creative spirit. I then think about my father again.

My father has all the talents of a great creative writer but chose to work in other fields. He comes from a long line of writers, directors, actors, and storytellers. I believe that we inherit talents from our ancestors and I think I have been deeply affected by my father simply because I sprang from his loins.

When I think of my father I can't help but think of my Maori mother, whose womb nurtured me and who gave birth to me. As a child I had more of a relationship with my mother than my father because he always worked long hours in order to pay the bills and put food on the table. Mum once won a prize at her rural school for writing about her pet pig when everyone else in the class wrote about their pet lambs. Quite a feat, I think, when I consider the fact that she thought in Maori as a girl and that writing in English was a struggle. My mother often told stories about my Maori history and culture and these have become like wells from which I draw much of my inspiration for writing.

My father has always sought to understand anything that seemed alien to him. After he married my mother, from the Ngati Porou tribe, both my parents opened up our house to all my Ngati Porou relations and all our Maori acquaintances, who frequently dropped in for a while as they passed through or stopped to stay for a year or two. Most of these people were very colourful characters with a terrific sense of humour. Apart from one man, who molested my baby sister, all of these people were extremely kind to us children. These Maori of my father's generation, who often lived with us, have done well in their lives. They've never forgotten how my father and mother opened up their home and lives to them. My stepmother was also from the Ngati Porou tribe, and I can say that

APIRANA TAYOR

JUSTINE LORD

in a sense my father has had a love affair with the Maori people, especially Ngati Porou people, for nearly 50 years.

It was my father who convinced my mother that I should be called Apirana, after Apirana Ngata. Dad encouraged my interest in Maori and nurtured my pride and love for my Maori people and culture. I was naturally inclined to think this way and his encouragement strengthened me and had a great effect on my life, my attitudes and my writing. When I was a child, Maori people, life, and culture were, to say the least, not held in high esteem at all by most Pakeha and my Pakeha father had a lot of vision and foresight in this respect. He was a man born before his time. He led protests against South Africa and apartheid in the 1950s long before most people ever thought about, or cared enough to protest against, that evil regime.

Dad has always had a real love and fascination for journalism. As Dad was a journalist, I can remember from an early age wanting to grow up and be a writer like him. He had and still has a newspaper editor's hatred for verbosity and he delights in words and well-written phrases. He writes very well. During his life he's written many interesting articles which still make good reading. In 1958 he wrote a booklet on Wai Whetu marae which is being reissued unchanged to this day. He won the Cowan prize for journalism in the early 1950s for writing an article

MELVIN
TAYOR

about race relations in Auckland. Dad's a talented man but, like you and me, he is not perfect.

My mother died when I was 11. Shortly after that Dad went overseas to further his career for 25 years. This meant that my relationship with my father during that time was mainly a long-distance one and basically I only ever saw him spasmodically, once or twice a year, for almost a quarter of a century. I visited him sometimes during the school holidays and he came back to New Zealand when work permitted. The positive side of this is that I saw a lot more of the world than most youngsters my age.

I've a vague memory of my father absent-mindedly speaking his thoughts out loud as he edited an article when I was a child. I remember mentally editing the same article and taking as much delight as he did in creating rich, powerful phrases with an economy of choice words.

Dad once congratulated me for winning a prize for an article I wrote as a teenager. He always encouraged me to better myself and do well. Throughout his life he's been a perfectionist. Everything for him must be planned down to the last dotted 'i' and crossed 't'. He can't stand the littlest speck of dust on his shoes or a pinprick of a spot on his tie. I've seen him get into a very bad mood if such things are not exactly right. I am not like this at all. I've got holes in most of my shoes and you can't see my old overalls because they are covered in paint stains. I've got Dad's mania for perfection in one thing and one thing only. I seek and accept nothing else but perfection in the poetry, short stories, novels, and plays that I write and also in the roles I play as an actor. To my father's horror and amazement, my attempts to organise the rest of my life seem vague, ramshackle, and muddled to him.

I've organised myself as best as I can to do what I want to do, which is write and act. I get angry and start yelling and throwing things when people make hopeless attempts to get me to organise the other parts of my life such as eating, paying bills or keeping a shelter over my head, which I show little interest in, although as a family man I've had to try and change this attitude.

Like any good journalist, my father is hounded by a nagging sense of curiosity. He's excessively inquisitive. Dad's sense of curiosity has often been a source of embarrassment to the rest of his family. When we were children, if any of our friends who Dad didn't know walked into the room, he would grill them with questions. He'd ask: Who are you? What are you? Where do you come from? How old are you? Who are your parents? How old are they? Why do you do this? Where did you get those shoes from, and why do you wear them? And who's your uncle? He can't help but pepper people with questions because he just has to know what's going on around him. I ask questions every day of my life, but my sense of curiosity is different from Dad's. I can know someone for years and still not know what their first name is unless someone shouts it in my ears loudly several times. Yet my nagging inquisitiveness is just as strong as Dad's – it's just of an introspective nature. I question the human condition – who, how, why, and what – and I constantly nag God, people, and society for answers.

In recent years my father has helped and inspired me in my chosen careers. He is the most knowledgeable man I've ever met when it comes to New Zealand literature. He seldom talks about it but when he does, I'd advise anybody to shut up and listen, which is what I do. I don't know where he got this knowledge from. He's never been to university. He's a well-read man and yet I've never seen him read a book.

I could be wrong but I've a suspicion Dad wanted all his children to be doctors and lawyers. None of my brothers and sisters are doctors or lawyers, we're all writers and actors. Dad says that in the end he just wants us to be what makes us happy.

I think my father is a very fine man. Like my mother, he never hit us when we were children although he was a stickler for discipline. He likes to tell a good story and he has a great sense of humour. He can captivate people and make them laugh for hours. There are many things about my father I would like to emulate, but there are one or two things he's done which I couldn't do. I don't ever intend to be an absent father for too long.

Dad is on medication now and he can hardly tie up his shoes or dress as immaculately, dapperly or perfectly as he's always liked to. Coping with his retirement is something he finds very difficult. I will never have the problem of retirement, since as a writer and actor I can, health permitting, keep writing and acting until the day I die, if I wish, and no one can ever force me to stop.

Unlike my father, who has been addicted to newspapers, I've seldom cared a fig for them. For most of my young adult life the only thing I ever read in newspapers was my stars and Charlie Brown since it seemed to me that only in these two things did newspapers get anywhere near the truth. Until recently I've never had any interest in writing for newspapers. My sole focus of energy as far as writing goes has always been to write plays, novels, short stories, and poetry.

My father is an honest and moral man. Much of his life has been a good example for me to try and follow. My early childhood was alcohol and violence free. I have both my parents to thank for that. I have lived in many different situations. I've lived in gutters one day and in palaces the next. I think I've lived a rich and full life. I feel I've seen a lot thus far and am a very fortunate man.

By the time I reach my father's age and have to go to hospitals for medication, I hope to be a wiser man than I am now. For I have my father's nagging curiosity, but rather than just wanting to know who you are or who I am, I also want to know who made us and why.

ONE O' THESE
BLOODY DAYS

PHILIP TEMPLE

I

'Begin the Beguine'. Played by Artie Shaw and his Orchestra. Not the original recording from July 1938 but the later version with strings. This is the first music I remember hearing. Probably in 1941, when I was two. Because he played it over and over, setting the 78 record in place on the radiogram in the recess to the left of the tiled fireplace. In the front room of the terraced house in the sloping street in Stanningley, near Pudsey (Len Hutton came from there) and Bradford. I still play Artie Shaw's 'Begin the Beguine'; from a collection called *Classic Bands of the '30s*. Pop, pop, pop with the remote control until I find the right band on the CD. Reviving the saccharine strings and lurching clarinet. Starting up my father's signature tune. His only enduring presence. If you were to ask me, I would have to say, yes, it remains one of my favourite tunes.

I have only two other memories of him from that time. Riding in our little car, my father with his elbow resting on the open window frame and my mother saying, 'One day you'll have it bloody knocked off.' And then the row. After he had hit me. Screaming as my mother drags me from the high chair and then clutches me in her arms while they circle around the settee. The anger, the fury; the shouting and banging. Then there came a special silence, the egregious silence of inexplicable absence. There are only women. In the house, in the streets, everywhere. I cling to my mother in the night when the guns explode and the cows in the fields beyond the railway line scream as falling shrapnel lacerates their flanks. Cling to the nurse in the hospital at the terrifying wail of the siren, the lights flickering and going out, clutching at her shoulder, hanging on to the model Spitfire, vomiting over her breast.

Men came again to the house but only in uniform. Strange men but brave men, smart in blue with white wings on their chests. They brought reassurance and I wanted one of them to come back: he made my Hornby train set work properly. He came back only once or twice, and the last time he stood on the train and broke it, as he was reaching up to close the blackout curtains. He promised to come and fix it but he never did. My mother said that he was never going to come back but she could not explain it properly, and I cried a lot, for myself, bitterly over the Hornby train, and for something else which she cried for, too, but which I could not understand except in feeling her grief; and the absence, the irrevocable absence.

I went to live with my Granny – my mother's mother – and her second coal-miner husband, Grandad Jim, at Castleford when I was four-and-a-half. I started school at Lock Lane Primary. By now I knew my father would not be coming back and that he didn't want to come back and my mother didn't want him to come back because he was no good and we were better off without him. What could I say? What could I think? Nothing. I had to be a brave boy. Everybody had to be brave at that time: I didn't have it on my own.

I didn't realise it, but my mother was very young, 19 when I was born. Later, I became aware that she was very good-looking – smashing – but never understood until I was adult that she had her own life to lead, separate from me. I could never understand why she had to be separate from me. First, she went up to London, for good, and I remember my utter misery and helplessness. She told me she had to go to London but that I couldn't go because of the bombing. It wasn't safe for children; it was safer to stay in Yorkshire. But I could go to London, too, when the bombing stopped. After the War. But that, I knew, was ages away.

While I was at my loving granny's, my other granny and my real grandad came round. My father's parents. I have written about this in my autobiographical novel *Sam* (1984). How a five or six year-old, at the mercy of adults, copes with the prejudice and emotional violence born of their ignorance and fear. Grandad Jim brutally prevented my father's parents from seeing me and abused them in my hearing with my father's unspecified sins:

> '*An' where's that dirty bloody son of yourn, eh?'*
>
> *'Can a see me other Granny?' His Granny stood in the doorway between the kitchen and the front room and held on to Sam's arm so he couldn't get past.*
>
> *'I 'aven't seen a brass farthing out of 'im these past six months!'*
>
> *'I want to see me other Granny!' Sam cried.*
>
> *'An' tha can tell that bloody stuck-up son of thine that if 'e bothers coming round 'ere again I'll break 'is bloody neck for 'im!' . . .*
>
> *Grandad shouting, 'I'll look after 'im a bloody sight better than that good for nothin' son o' thine! Aye, an' don't tha bother comin' back either! Arse'oles to thee as well!' And he slammed the front door so hard one of the plates slipped off its stand on the sideboard.*

When my Granny remonstrated with him, 'An' tha shouldn't talk like that in front of the lad,' he replied: 'Why not? 'E'll find out one o' these bloody days.'

Closeted in my room soon after, the cover of my old 1924 Tiger Tim's Annual fell open and I saw the writing on the inside.

> *It was his father's name and address at Wellgate, written out just like Sam would write it out. Sam looked at it for a minute and then he picked up a stub of pencil from the floor and wrote, 'Ha! Ha! Ha!' underneath and then he scribbled all over it, round and round and round, until he couldn't read anything at all.*

Grandad Jim was right: I would 'find out one o' these bloody days', but he would never have thought that day would be 40 years off. Everything to do with my father was shut down. I never saw or heard from my paternal grandparents again. Later, the only reference to my father came when my mother regularly stood me against the wall and told me to stand up straight while she checked that my legs were both the same length. My father, she said, had one leg shorter than the other and she was going to make sure I didn't have the same affliction. At these times, I would tentatively ask about him. She would always say that he did a terrible thing – a *disgusting* thing. Her voice would rise and sometimes

PHILIP WITH HIS MOTHER, PATERNAL GRANDMOTHER AND FATHER

her face would become red and suffused with loathing and she would become angry at my even asking. She had a terrible temper. I felt guilty. My deformed, *disgusting* father was someone to be ashamed of. So I shut him out and yearned for another one.

My first father-substitute was my mother's long-dead father, Alf. She spoke of him often, in a worshipful way, eyes glistening with fond emotion, pride in her voice as she described to me his manifold virtues. He had died of tuberculosis at the age of 31 in 1927, when she had been seven years old. He had been a seaman in submarines during the First World War and a coal miner. He hadn't had a chance. She told me he had always worked for better conditions for his fellow workers and had gone to prison for standing up for their rights. (From a *Yorkshire Post* clipping, many years later, I discovered that in 1919 he had stood on a soap box in Castleford market place and preached a Soviet revolution. He had been jailed for six months for sedition.) My mother told me that he had been a great entertainer, with a wonderful natural musical talent; he played several instruments, composed songs and appeared at the Castleford Music Hall; once he had taken her on stage with him. He would have been famous if he had lived.

This working-class hero came to my immediate rescue. My mother took me to a spiritualist meeting in Kensington, soon after I joined her in London in 1946, aged seven. A medium passed on messages to members of the congregation after a church service:

'Is that small boy with you?' the white lady said to Sam's Mum.

His Mum cleared her throat slightly and said in a very clear voice, 'Yes, he is.'

'You're his mother?'

'I am.'

The white lady closed her eyes and Sam didn't dare move. He felt his face going red but he shivered a bit because it felt as if a draught was blowing down the back of his neck.

'There's a man standing behind your son,' the white lady said slowly. 'He's dressed in a sailor's uniform and has very striking blue eyes. Do you know who it is?'

'Yes, I do,' his Mum said.

'He says not to worry about . . . about Sam, is it? . . . because he'll look after him.'

It was my real grandad! My mother had shown me the one photo she had of him – in a sailor's uniform and he had bright blue eyes!

Dead Grandfather Alf became my guardian angel. I believed with all the uncomplicated trust and deep fervour of a small child that this hero would be with me, no matter where I went, what I did or what happened to me. The medium had passed me an emotional lifeline; and reinforced my mother's insistence that I was a special child, with qualities inherited from Alf that would see me go far. This also served to further obliterate my father. Physically, emotionally and intellectually I was hers and her father's. No-one else counted.

Alf looked after me well. I would curl up at night and talk to him, ask him for advice, protection or help, and feel comforted when I was being bullied at school in Notting Hill for my Yorkshire accent or when it seemed I could never satisfy my mother's demands. Above all, when I was heartbroken at being sent by her to a boarding school at the age of eight; and when I found myself in desperate straits on running away from it (10 times).

Can you hear me? Can you hear me? You said you'd look after me. You said you would. What am I going to do? What am I going to do? He talked and he talked and he talked and he beat against the tree with his fists and tore off pieces of bark and kicked at the tree roots and he went on and on and on until he noticed that the rain was no longer dropping on his head and he looked out from under the tree to see that the rain had almost stopped. Away to his right there was a weak flashing of sunlight low in the trees.

On that runaway, I gave Alf thanks before sleeping in a bed made of sacks I had discovered in an orchard shed.

But Alf was not enough, of course. I wanted a real father, urgently, all the time. At the boarding school, I was not reconciled to having an absent solo mum by the fact that all the boys around me were also without fathers – lost in the war. There was a general sense of misery, of loss, of separation from mothers that simply exacerbated my self-pity. I was also aware that I hadn't lost my father in the war in the way the other boys' fathers had been lost – shot down over Hamburg, incinerated in a tank at Tobruk or sunk in a destroyer in mid-Atlantic. My father had just disappeared, and my mother told me not to talk about it if the subject ever came up with the other boys. Somehow she had fudged the application form for the school, an entirely charitable institution, so that she could get me in. It had been an act of desperation. She was chronically poor and at the time could not see how to earn enough money to look after me. Grandad Jim had made it brutally clear she could not send me back to Yorkshire. The hatred between them was palpable.

Her poverty, my constant running away from boarding school, and my pathetic need for a father, were major factors in driving my mother to find a second husband. I remember a well-spoken man coming to take her out, from the house in Bayswater where we lived in an attic room. She tried to avoid my seeing him, but I slipped the baby-sitter. Would he be my new father? I remember the cut and smell of good tweed, the briefness of the encounter as my mother – who really did look smashing that night in her best make-up and clothes – took him away. I never saw him again; but in later years she told me that he had asked her to marry him and she had been tempted because he came from a good family, was well-off, and would have been able to send me to the right schools. But she didn't love him. Love! I'm glad I knew nothing of this at the time.

Towards the end of my time at boarding school, my mother met a handsome Anglo-Burmese man who had just been demobbed from the RAF and was living in the small private hotel where she worked. They were both 28 and she did love him. She must have decided that this was going to be the right marriage – though he was engaged to someone else – when she carefully introduced us to each other while I was on holiday from the school.

He was charming, he was kind, he was dashing with wonderfully black Brylcreemed hair like Denis Compton, and he was what every small boy wanted in a father at the time. He had been in the RAF during the War and had been shot down over Germany. He wore the little wriggly badge which showed that he had parachuted out and was entitled to belong to the Caterpillar Club. He had been a rear gunner in a Halifax bomber, which was a bit disappointing since the *crème de la crème* would have been a Spitfire pilot; but he had probably shot down a night fighter. All of this was so important in school pecking orders.

For the first time, in Kensington Gardens, I experienced horseplay with a father figure. It was both exhilarating and frightening; and captivating. Soon I worshipped him and my terrible, weeping entreaties, when he seemed to be going off to join his fiancée, were crucial to his decision to come back for my mother. She had managed the situation well.

My mother and stepfather were married in May 1948 and I came back from boarding school to live happily ever after with them in a basement flat in Bayswater. I have a snap of my stepfather from about this time with my pencilled, childish caption on the back which confirmed my familial state: 'Dad in Kensington Gardens'. I was happy and proud to change my second name.

Things altered a year later when my stepbrother was born and my brief tenure at the centre of the small family was abruptly ended. Fatherless for so long, I now had to share his affections. Worse, I detected soon that this was his *real* son who had a *real* father. My stepfather's kindness and dependability could not disguise and compensate for this. Also, I had revealed to this swimming and tennis champion of a minor public school that I was a physical coward and shied away from sports. I began to earn his amused contempt.

The honeymoon was over and my first response was to do what I had successfully done before. I ran away from home, Alf riding shotgun. I was

PHILIP WITH HIS STEPFATHER

going off to be a Swallow in Arthur Ransome's Lake District and bought a train ticket, with money meant for groceries, which took me about a quarter of the way. After a couple of nights' sleeping out in wintry weather, I gave myself up at a country police station. We all had to readjust.

In the years that followed, as I went on to grammar school and we moved to a council house on an estate outside London and then back in to a council flat in Chelsea, I had the day-to-day security of a father, the structure of a family. I grew to love my stepbrother but found that I had less and less in common with my stepfather, who seemed to become more and more taciturn, undemonstrative and only reluctantly interested in what was essential to my life. At times, it seemed that my mother also suffered emotional deprivation in her relationship with him and turned too often to me with her thoughts and feelings and dreams, relying on my unquestioning devotion and the deep bonds between us. She was ambitious for me, and for my stepfather who, much to her frustration, seemed content to plod on with clerical work in the headquarters of a major office equipment firm in the city. At times, inexcusably, she used me as an ally to try and manipulate him into doing what she wanted. This was rarely productive and largely served to increase the tension and distance between my stepfather and me. He began to see me as a rival for her affections.

The denouement came when I was 15. My mother increasingly disapproved of my stepfather spending hours at the pub with his office friends on Friday evenings. She told me that it was a terrible waste of our scarce income and a dangerous habit. I was too naive and self-righteous to think there was a good deal more to it than that. She put me up to saying something to him when he returned late one Friday evening, the worse for several pints. Not surprisingly, he knocked me down. Now there could never be anything between us.

I left school at 17 in 1956. I wanted to leave home. Everything that my mother had done for me had been meant for the best; but I needed to escape her emotional dominance. I wanted to escape the country, too, and its climate of constant economic crisis and collapsing empire, not to mention its imminent demand that I give up two years of my life to military service just when I needed to define my independence. The idea of travel appealed, but I had no money. The solution to all of this was to become a '10 pound Pom' and go to New Zealand. So I ran away again, as far as I could go, and left mother, father, stepfather and all that austere and uncomfortable childhood behind. It was a clean, exhilarating but deeply painful break. Alf was not much use in helping me adjust to the rugby-muscled, half-gallon quarter acres of 1950s New Zealand. But it was not possible to go back. I had to and did become a New Zealander. There is not room here to describe how that happened, except to say that it entailed, for more than a decade, the burial of my past.

II

In 1969 my stepbrother, and then in 1970 my mother and stepfather, followed me out to New Zealand. By then I was married and had an infant daughter and son. My wife and children were all New Zealanders and, in 1970, I formally became a New Zealand citizen myself. My stepbrother went to Taupo and stayed; my parents remained six years in Auckland and then returned to England. I was in Wellington until 1972, before shifting to Banks Peninsula. Family relationships were always uncomfortable: distances in space, time, personality, and experience meant that we were no longer close and little of the past was explored or settled.

As my children began to grow, in a family environment that I was determined would be better than mine had been – emotionally and physically secure – the place and role of their grandparents had to be addressed. I had not given my real father much thought for many years; my mother's propaganda during my childhood, and the chasm between my current and past lives, had almost erased him. But the need I saw to complete the familial picture for my children, in conjunction with the more objective views I had developed of my mother during her years in New Zealand, released me at last from the thrall in which she had held me for more than 30 years. Nearing 40, I finally asked myself, without tremor or distaste, who was my father? What was he like? What did we have in common? What had he done? Where was he now? I needed to find out, before it was too late.

In 1979, I travelled with my family to England, returning after an absence of 22 years. One of my chief objects was to find my father. It was awkward, broaching the subject with my mother. The old tensions were still there, but she accepted my need to find out and, tacitly, the impossibility of deterring me. She volunteered no information but, genuinely, had no idea where he might be.

We went to Yorkshire and stayed with friends near Bradford where, at the town hall, we were given good advice about tracing relatives. After one or two false starts, we realised that the most effective way to find my father was to locate *his* father's death certificate, which would probably include my father's address among the details of next of kin. Neighbours in Castleford confirmed that my paternal grandfather had continued to live at his home in Glasshoughton until his death, long after his wife had died. Amazingly, one couple recalled that he had died about 20 years before and remembered seeing a man, whom they took to be his son, visiting the house to settle his affairs. Since we couldn't find a death certificate at the appropriate local office, we searched a funeral director's records and there found a burial certificate with my grandfather's place of death given as Goole, in east Yorkshire. He had died while on a visit to a friend.

I remember speeding down the highways to reach the office of the Registrar of Births, Deaths and Marriages in Goole before it closed at noon on a Wednesday, and excitedly scanning the copy of my grandfather's death certificate which showed that he, a retired journeyman plumber, had died in 1959 at the age of 81. And there was the name and Bradford address of my father. But we knew already that he was not in the Bradford phone book; he must have moved on. We drove rapidly back, introduced ourselves as my father's long-lost friends from New Zealand to the current occupants of the house in Bradford and found that he and his second wife had moved to a place near Chorley in Lancashire a year or two before. We came away with his address and phone number. It had taken just three days.

After his initial incomprehension, my father responded to my phone call with astonishing phlegm. 'You'd better come over then,' he said in a flat, matter-of-fact Yorkshire way. The next day, I drove across the Pennines to Lancashire and found him without trouble, waiting in the garden outside his bungalow; and we knew each other on sight without question. I was 40 and he was 63. On reflection, I guess he must have known it would happen one day and his only surprise might have been that it had taken so long. But he showed no surprise or apprehension; neither joy nor resentment. He and his wife were hospitable, cautious and, above all, curious about why I had come. The most interest they expressed was in my children, their instant grand-children, because their married son and only child had yet to produce. So I had found a new stepbrother, too; 10 years younger than me, the same age as my other stepbrother. Directly after receiving my phone call the day before, my father had called him saying, 'There's something important I must come over to talk to you about.'

They relaxed when it became apparent that I had not come to make material claims. But my father's wife seemed always within earshot when I was alone with him, on that first occasion and on every other occasion when I was able to visit them in the years that followed. Perhaps she was on hand in case I pushed him too hard about what had happened between him and my mother; either because she knew or because she hoped to discover more.

Within the first hour, I was startled by the physical similarities between myself and my father. The way we scratched our noses and the backs of our necks. Now I could see where my hair came from, and my psoriasis, though his was very much worse. His limp confirmed what my mother had told me long before, and his early introduction into the conversation of motor cars and pride in his DIY mechanical skills chimed with my dim memory of the little car and his elbow jutting from the driver's window. He was disappointed I had no interest in mechanics and even more disappointed to learn that I had changed my surname and taken my mother's choice of first name and not his, which he had given me after his grandfather. My gladness at finding him, my curiosity to learn more, was overcome by a brief surge of resentment, contempt even. What had he done to deserve my keeping his names? Why had he never made any attempt to find me?

We sat at the dining table for several hours, exchanging information about ourselves. He had gained enough training at night school as a teenager to become an engineer's draughtsman, working before the war on armoured cars for General Electric in Bradford and then shifting to Avro at Yeadon where he had been part of the team working on the design and construction of the famous Lancaster bomber. After the war, he had worked for manufacturing companies, and had progressed into lower management. Before he retired he had supervised the closing down of textile factories when the Lancashire industry failed under the onslaught of Asian competition.

He had a mild interest in local history and he and his wife had taken to participating in antique fairs as a social hobby. He liked a pint or two, liked taking the occasional holiday in southern Germany, liked pottering with motor cars. He had no other enthusiasm, though that word is too strong to append to anything he did or said. I had difficulty discovering anything other than physical similarities between us, even after we had met several times: perhaps his method and attention to detail, an occasional caustic scepticism, but not much else.

My father was grey-haired, bespectacled, overweight, and sedentary. His son said that he would rather spend half an hour finding or waiting for a parking place within a hundred yards of his destination than walk any distance, although given his leg that seemed unkind. When I spoke to him of my writing and photography and mountaineering, and of recently leading a trekking group to the Mount Everest region, his reaction was a curious mixture of incomprehension, suppressed admiration, and shame. My father had led a colourless and mediocre life, perhaps beset by E. M. Forster's 'quiet desperation', if he had known the passion even for that.

About 10 years after first meeting my father, I spent an evening in the pub with my 'new' stepbrother. He took after his mother, had done well in the police force in the computer field, and seemed happily married and at home in North Yorkshire. After a few pints, which he sank with deceptive rapidity, he asked me, 'How d'you get on with him, then?'

I shrugged: 'All right. We don't have a lot in common but . . .' It did not seem sensible to say, 'Well, he's my father. I just need to visit him whenever I have the opportunity . . .' I couldn't explain it beyond knowing that a vacancy in my life had been filled by finding him and hearing of his life, especially of those years before I had a stepfather; and that I had a deep, atavistic need to be, for the first time in my life, close to my father, no matter who he was or what he represented. Like a cat or a dog that has been far removed from its original home, I had been driven, instinctively, to find my way back. But then this had brought my unconscious anguish to the surface: how could he have forgotten his son?

My stepbrother took another deep draught of beer and became vehement. 'Well, you missed *nothing*,' he said. 'He was no father at all to me. He took no interest in me or my schooling. Whenever I came home he was always under his car. The only thing he ever had any interest in was his bloody car. If I ever wanted to talk to him about something personal, something really important to me, he just made a joke of it. Shied away. You know, he didn't know how to deal with that sort of thing.' He ordered another pint. 'He's never had the character.' There was nothing more to be said.

My father admitted to me that I had been better off with my mother; that I'd never have done what I had if I'd lived with him. In admitting his inadequacy, he employed it as an excuse for having taken no responsibility for me. I tried and tried on that first visit to ask him why he had never looked for me. But it choked in my throat, for I suspected it was simply because he couldn't be bothered. And the child in me didn't want to face that. But one day, calmly, he said, 'I did try to find you, you know. When I was down in London, I looked in the phone book. But it was no good . . . and it was difficult, anyway, because your mother . . . well . . . she wanted to cut things off . . . I couldn't . . .' He shook his head. His excuse was so pathetic any feelings of distress I may have had were overcome by disbelief and a kind of contemptuous pity.

Later, I considered how difficult it would have been for a man like this to stand up to the emotional manipulations and explosive rages of my mother. She had recounted to me, more than once, that she had told him – and I could imagine the fire and the anger of her uncompromising declaration – that she did not want a penny from him for my upkeep so long as he never made any attempt to see either of us ever again. Any urges he may have had to see me as a child would have been quickly suppressed by contemplation of the immense difficulties he would have had in persuading my mother to give him access. In the tradition of the Lock Lane coal-miner families – just as Grandad Jim had shut out my father's parents – she would have slammed the door in his face after shouting a close equivalent to Jim's 'Arse'oles to thee!'

I hesitated also to ask him the other burning question. Why did he and my mother split? What *disgusting* thing did he do? While I had some right to know, I was reluctant to invade the privacy of someone I did not yet know very well.

But it hung in the air from the beginning and, again, he took it upon himself to offer an explanation . . .

In the early years of the war, the need arising from the national emergency to produce quickly an effective heavy bomber to hit back at Germany demanded that Avro work round the clock to get the Lancaster into the air. My father worked 12-hour shifts for months on end with just one day off a week. He told me how in the winter of 1940–41 he would get up in the dark, cycle several miles to Yeadon where he worked under artificial lights in the giant Avro hangar (its roof camouflaged with earth, trees, and mock cows), and then cycle home again in the dark, completely exhausted. He said that this stressful working life was the cause of the deepening conflicts with my mother that finally led to their separation and divorce.

I could tell that this was only part of the story but I could not ask for more. Once, when we went out to a pub for Sunday lunch, he leaned across the bar and began to say, 'You know, this business about your mother and me . . .', and I could tell from his expression that he was about to tell me at least part of the *disgusting* secret. But so could his wife, who swiftly joined us and interrupted the conversation.

I had to wait until after his death in 1992 to learn the secret. It was as if my mother felt freed by this event; and, perhaps, she had not wanted to disturb the relationship I had with him while he was alive. Now she could tell me that he had consorted with a prostitute and had contracted gonorrhoea. This was the *disgusting* secret which had grown enormous in my imagination and consequently now seemed trivial in the telling, especially in the generation of AIDS. But such an event, even in the 1990s, would be enough to destroy most intimate relationships. In the early 1940s, especially among working class people, it was the ultimate marital crime, desperately shaming to all involved, something to be hidden at all costs, to be swept away, and for me to be protected from. Here was my father's ultimate weakness, another powerful reason why he would have felt himself unable to lay any sort of claim to me. Better the clean break, and a moving on to new lives.

Naturally, I wondered why my father had felt the need to go with prostitutes. I could only imagine the nature of the relationship between my mother and father. They had been, after all, so young: 18 and just 21 when they married. Reversing the generational perspective, I could have only compassion for this couple young enough to be my children. Poorly educated children; poorly nourished children of the Depression; both only children in socially narrow circumstances; ignorant sexually; and then placed under the immense pressures of a national emergency that no one could escape. Finally, I had found out 'one o' these bloody days'. And I could understand, accept and forgive.

I discharged much of my anguish and resolved much of my buried childhood trauma in the catharsis of writing *Sam* in 1981. This, written almost automatically, was ignited by finding my father and by visiting my childhood landscapes in 1979. Alf finally left me when I finished that book and he stayed away for a dozen years, until after my father's death, when he slowly returned, and remains, if at a distance. Because he is my real paternal hero.

Because if you were to ask me, I would say, no, I never had a father. I do not wish to depreciate the responsible care of my stepfather; I am grateful that he was there during my later childhood. But I had no father in the sense of a man who had a son whom he regarded as his own; whom he cherished and cared for, no matter how imperfectly, from when that son was born until he was grown. I know I am far from alone in not having had this kind of father; I became aware of this first before I ran away from boarding school, and was always told to be brave about it. The trouble is that no matter how distant the events of my childhood become; no matter how much I know, understand and accept; no matter how much I rationalise or forgive, the child in me still cries out, 'Why did he never come and find me?'

Biographical Notes

Murray Ball was born in 1939 in Feilding. He and his wife Pam live near Gisborne on a 220-hectare hill-country farm. They have three grown-up children. He has worked as a cartoonist for the *Manawatu Times*, the *Dominion*, *Punch*, and the *Labour Weekly* but is best known as the creator of *Footrot Flats*, as well as the internationally syndicated *Stanley the Paleolithic Hero*. He also wrote and directed the full-length animated feature film, *Footrot Flats: The Dog's Tale*. Although he no longer draws the syndicated strip, he continues to work on the Footrot Flats books which include *The Ballad of Footrot Flats*, a full-length story in verse. He produces two new books of Footrot Flats strips each year, and these have sold more than six million copies. In addition, he writes and illustrates satirical books on contemporary New Zealand. Murray Ball has also been a successful rugby player, representing Manawatu from 1958–62 and being selected as a Junior All Black in 1959 and as an All Black triallist in 1960.

Rupert Glover was born in 1945 in Christchurch and has had successful careers as both a filmmaker and lawyer. After graduating MA (Hons) from Canterbury University in 1968, he tutored in English then worked for the National Film Unit where he became a director. During these years he produced two collections of poems, *The Wine and the Garlic* and (together with Stephen Chan and Merlene Young) *Postcards from Paradise*. In 1972 he moved to Canada, where he was employed as a film editor for Radio Canada and a film producer for the National Film Board of Canada. His films have won a number of international awards. After returning to New Zealand in 1978, he studied law at Canterbury University, graduating LLB with first-class honours in 1981. He has lectured in law at Canterbury but is now in private practice in Christchurch. He has been president of the Criminal Bar Association of Canterbury and is an author of the textbook *Acts Interpretation* (1991).

Bryan Gould was born in Hawera in 1939. He studied law at both Victoria University of Wellington and Auckland University before going to Balliol College, Oxford, as a Rhodes Scholar in 1961. He graduated from Oxford with a BCL in 1964 and joined the British diplomatic service, leaving in 1968 to tutor in law at Worcester College, Oxford. In 1974, he won the seat of Southampton Test for Labour, but lost it in the Conservative victory of 1979. In 1983, he contested Dagenham and held it until his resignation in 1994. He rose rapidly in the opposition Labour Party to become a member of the Shadow Cabinet and made an unsuccessful leadership bid in 1992. His years in British politics were marked by his consistent opposition to monetarism and the federalising tendencies of the European Union. In 1994, he returned to New Zealand as Vice-Chancellor of the University of Waikato. He has also worked as a television presenter and has published several books, including *Socialism and Freedom* and an autobiography, *Goodbye to All That*.

Chris Laidlaw was born in 1943 in Dunedin and has had a distinguished career both in sport and in public life. He represented Otago at rugby, swimming, water polo and surfing, but is best known as an All Black from 1963–1970 (captain in 1968). He later opposed sporting links with South Africa and came into conflict with Prime Minister Muldoon. His book *Mud in Your Eye* (1973) is a candid and at times humorous analysis of the state of the game in the early 1970s. He was educated at Otago University and at Oxford, where he was a Rhodes scholar and graduated in 1971 with a BLitt in anthropology and geography. From 1972–1989 he worked for the Ministry of Foreign Affairs, with postings to Suva, Paris, Bonn, and London, eventually becoming the first New Zealand ambassador in southern Africa, based in Harare. From 1989–1992 he was the race relations conciliator and, after a brief stint as MP for Wellington Central, in 1994 he was appointed executive director of the World Wide Fund for Nature NZ.

Owen Marshall is one of New Zealand's foremost short fiction writers and has published eight short story collections. He is also the author of a novel (*A Many Coated Man*, 1995) and a radio play, and the editor of three anthologies of New Zealand writing. The many awards for his fiction include the University of Canterbury Literary Fellowship, the

New Zealand Literary Fund Scholarship in Letters, the Robert Burns Fellowship at the University of Otago, and the Katherine Mansfield Memorial Fellowship in 1996. Born in Te Kuiti in 1941, Marshall was for many years a teacher, but in 1985 he resigned as acting rector of Waitaki Boys' High School, Oamaru, to devote more time to writing, which has increasingly been his occupation, although he still runs a fiction writing course for part of each year at Aoraki Polytechnic, Timaru. He has spent almost all his life in South Island towns and has an affinity with provincial New Zealand.

Greg Newbold is a senior lecturer in sociology at Canterbury University. In 1975, as a young university student, he was arrested for heroin trafficking and sentenced to seven-and-a-half years' imprisonment. In prison he studied for an MA degree and won first class honours with a thesis on the social organisation of prisons. After his release near the end of 1980, Newbold studied at Auckland University for his PhD, which was awarded in 1987. In the following year, he joined the staff of Canterbury University. Newbold has written three books on crime and criminal justice in New Zealand and one on the history of the New Zealand Association of the Blind. He has published numerous articles in these areas, frequently comments on such matters in the media, and is often contracted by government to advise or conduct research on crime and criminal justice matters. In 1990 he won the Lilian Ida Smith short story award for an article on capital punishment.

Nicholas Reid, the youngest of the seven children of John and Joyce Reid, was born in November 1951. Married with seven children, he pays the mortgage by being a secondary school teacher, but has also gained steady employ over the last two decades as a critic and occasional broadcaster. For 10 years he was sole film reviewer for the *Auckland Star*, and he currently writes for *North and South* magazine. His book, *A Decade of New Zealand Film* (1986), was the first full-length study of the revived New Zealand cinema, and he has also published a monograph on Shakespeare's *Othello*. Seeing films, reviewing, raising a family, and teaching take up most of his time, but latterly he has acquired the hobby of doing an honours degree in church history.

Harry Ricketts was born in London in 1950. He grew up in England, Malaysia and Hong Kong and read English at Oxford University. Before coming to live in New Zealand in 1981, he taught at the universities of Hong Kong and Leicester and is now a senior lecturer in the English Department at Victoria University. His poems and critical essays have appeared in journals in New Zealand, Australia, Hong Kong, France, and England. His publications include a collection of short stories, *People Like Us* (1977), a book of interviews with New Zealand poets, *Talking About Ourselves* (1986), and four collections of poems, of which the most recent are *How Things Are* and *A Brief History of New Zealand Literature*, both published in 1996. He lives in Wellington and is currently writing a biography of Rudyard Kipling.

Peter Russell is associate professor of German at Victoria University. Born in Invercargill in 1945 and educated in Christchurch and Dunedin, he has also held university positions in Germany and Britain. He is the author of *The Divided Mind: A Portrait of Modern German Culture* (1988) and *Light in Battle with Darkness: Mahler's Kindertotenlieder* (1991), as well as numerous articles on aspects of nineteenth- and twentieth-century German literature. Also well known in New Zealand as a singer, specialising in lieder, he combines academic and musical interests in research and publication, lectures, seminars and radio talks, and in recital; and he has performed at international academic congresses in New Zealand, Germany, and Canada. Married with two children, he enjoys reading, music, and gardening.

Bill Sewell, born in 1951, came to New Zealand from England at the age of 14 and has lived here ever since, apart from a year spent in Germany in 1975–76. In 1978 he obtained a doctorate for work on the poetry of Hans Magnus Enzensberger from the University of Otago, where he also lectured in German for some years. A poet himself, he was Robert Burns Fellow at Otago in both 1981 and 1982. He then worked as a book editor in Dunedin before moving to Wellington in 1988, where in the following year he took up the study of law at Victoria University. Until early 1997 he was a legal researcher at the Law Commission in Wellington. He has published three collections of poems, as well as a number of articles and reviews in New Zealand and overseas journals.

Tony Simpson was born in Rangiora in 1945. Since graduating from Canterbury University he has worked variously as a radio producer, an arts administrator, trade union advocate, and public sector policy analyst and strategic planner. He lives mostly in Wellington, with which he has a longtime love affair, but admits to sometimes living in other people's countries. He is the author of a number of books of social history, including *The Sugarbag Years* and, most recently, *The Immigrants*, an account of emigration to New Zealand from Britain in the nineteenth century.

Apirana Taylor was born in 1955. He is of the Ngati Porou, Te Whanau a Apanui, Nga Puhi, Ngati Ruanui, and also Ngati Pakeha, tribes. Apirana opted out of university in the early 1970s in order to write poetry. Since then he has worked as a scrubcutter, fisherman, student journalist, freezing worker, carpenter, teacher's aid, producer of resources for education, and actor. For the past three or four years Apirana has been trying to live and support his family solely off the fruits of his art. His publications include three books of poetry, *The Eyes of the Ruru*, *Three Shades*, and *Soft Leaf Falls of the Moon*; two books of short stories, *He Rau Aroha*, and *Ki Te Ao*, which were published nationally and internationally by Penguin; and a novel, *He Tangi Aroha*. Apirana has also written several award-winning plays. He is currently acting in the film *Moby Dick*. In 1996 Apirana was writer in residence at Massey University, where he completed *Soft Leaf Falls of the Moon* and prepared his third collection of short stories for publication.

Philip Temple was born in Yorkshire in 1939 and educated at grammar schools in or near London before emigrating to New Zealand in 1957. Between 1959 and 1968 he was a mountaineer, explorer, and outdoor instructor. He made the first ascent of New Guinea's highest mountain in 1962. Between 1968 and 1972 he was the features editor for the *Listener* before becoming a full-time author. He was also associate editor of *Landfall* for some years. Since 1962, he has published more than 30 books, including the novels *Beak of the Moon*, *Dark of the Moon* and *Sam*; notable non-fiction works such as *The World At Their Feet* and *New Zealand Explorers*, photographic books and walking track guide books. Currently, he is working on a major biography of the Wakefield brothers. His work has been recognised by the award of the Katherine

Mansfield Fellowship in Menton (1979), the Robert Burns Fellowship (1980), a Berliner Künstlerprogramm Fellowship (1987), the Arts Council Non-Fiction Bursary (1994) and the National Library Research Fellowship (1996). He has two children and lives in Dunedin.